THE YOSEMITE NATIONAL PARK.

by John Muir

Of all the mountain ranges I have climbed, I like the Sierra Nevada the best. Though extremely rugged, with its main features on the grandest scale in height and depth, it is nevertheless easy of access and hospitable; and its marvelous beauty, displayed in striking and alluring forms, wooes the admiring wanderer on and on, higher and higher, charmed and enchanted. Benevolent, solemn, fateful, pervaded with divine light, every landscape glows like a countenance hallowed in eternal repose; and every one of its living creatures, clad in flesh and leaves, and every crystal of its rocks, whether on the surface shining in the sun or buried miles deep in what we call darkness, is throbbing and pulsing with the heartbeats of God. All the world lies warm in one heart, yet the Sierra seems to get more light than other mountains. The weather is mostly sunshine embellished with magnificent storms, and nearly everything shines from base to summit, — the rocks, streams, lakes, glaciers, irised falls, and the forests of silver fir and silver pine.

And how bright is the shining after summer showers and dewy nights, and after frosty nights in spring and autumn when the morning sunbeams are pouring through the crystals on the bushes and grass, and in winter through the snow-laden trees! The average cloudiness for the whole year is perhaps less than ten hundredths. Scarcely a day of all the summer is dark, though there is no lack of magnificent thundering cumuli. They rise in the warm midday hours, mostly over the middle region, in June and July, like new mountain ranges, higher Sierras, mightily augmenting the grandeur of the scenery while giving rain to the forests and gardens and bringing forth their fragrance. The wonderful weather and beauty inspire everybody to be up and doing. Every summer day is a workday to be confidently counted on, the short dashes of rain forming, not interruptions, but rests. The big blessed storm days of winter, when the whole range stands white, are not a whit less inspiring and kind. Well may the Sierra be called the Range of Light, not the Snowy Range; for only in winter is it white, while all the year it is bright.

Of this glorious range the Yosemite National Park is a central section, thirty-six miles in length and forty-eight miles in breadth. The famous Yosemite Valley lies in the heart of it, and it includes the head waters of the Tuolumne and Merced rivers, two of the most songful streams in the world; innumerable lakes and waterfalls and smooth silky lawns; the noblest forests, the loftiest granite domes, the deepest ice-sculptured cañons, the brightest crystalline pavements, and snowy mountains soaring into the sky twelve and thirteen thousand feet, arrayed in open ranks and spiry pinnacled groups partially separated by tremendous cañons and amphitheatres; gardens on their sunny brows, avalanches thundering down their long white slopes, cataracts roaring gray and foaming in the crooked

THE NORTH DOME.

rugged gorges, and glaciers in their shadowy recesses working in silence, slowly completing their sculpture; newborn lakes at their feet, blue and green, free or encumbered with drifting icebergs like miniature Arctic Oceans, shining, sparkling, calm as stars.

Nowhere will you see the majestic operations of nature more clearly revealed beside the frailest, most gentle and peaceful things. Nearly all the park is a profound solitude. Yet it is full of charming company, full of God's thoughts, a place of peace and safety amid the most exalted grandeur and eager enthusiastic action, a new song, a place of beginnings abounding in first lessons on life, mountain-building, eternal, invincible, unbreakable order; with sermons in stones, storms, trees, flowers, and animals brimful of humanity. During the last glacial period, just past, the former features of the range were rubbed off as a chalk sketch from a blackboard, and a new beginning was made. Hence the wonderful clearness and freshness of the rocky pages.

But to get all this into words is a hopeless task. The leanest sketch of each feature would need a whole chapter. Nor would any amount of space, however industriously scribbled, be of much avail. To defrauded town toilers, parks in magazine articles are like pictures of bread to the hungry. I can write only hints to incite good wanderers to come to the feast.

While this glorious park embraces big, generous samples of the very best of the Sierra treasures, it is, fortunately, at the same time, the most accessible portion. It lies opposite San Francisco, at a distance of about one hundred and forty miles. Railroads connected with all the continent reach into the foothills, and three good carriage roads, from Big Oak Flat, Coulterville, and Raymond, run into Yosemite Valley. Another, called the Tioga road, runs from Crocker's Station on the Yosemite Big Oak Flat road, near the

OUR YOSEMITE NATIONAL PARK

—among its forests and wild gardens, animals and birds, fountains and streams

by John Muir

EDITOR'S PREFACE

SOUTH OR HALF DOME.

At the turn of the century, John Muir described the Yosemite National Park in a series of articles to the readers of *Atlantic Monthly*. He was a fitting choice for an author, for just a decade before he had been so involved with the park idea that he became known as the "father of Yosemite National Park". But even if that had not been the case, he still would have been the best choice for the *Atlantic's* series—he knew the park better than anyone else and had a gift for expression that keeps his fame and his works alive yet.

When Muir originally wrote these articles (now the chapters in this book), Yosemite was a larger park than it is today, and consequently he describes some of the land to the east of the Sierra Nevada crest. Little matter, though, for that country is now set aside for similar uses in national forests and remains popular for wilderness hiking, climbing, and backpacking, which was his hope.

The writing here is perhaps the best blend Muir gave of the Yosemite as a wild nature preserve. The ecological account is full, and we learn much of Muir's observations of the Yosemite birds, bears, and blossoms as well as its winters, earthquakes, glaciers, and forests.

Until this edition, these chapters have been seen only once since they appeared in *The Atlantic Monthly*. Muir inserted them along with others on national parks into his 1901 book *Our National Parks*, which has long been out of print.

As this collection has not formerly been published separately, we have combined Muir's title for the lead article ("The Yosemite National Park") with that for the book in which they later appeared (*Our National Parks*), as *Our Yosemite National Park*. This should help identify it from his later and entirely separate work, *The Yosemite*.

To enhance the articles, we have added illustrations contemporary to their first appearance, from the following sources, several of which Muir wrote or edited: *Picturesque California* (1888), *Scribner's Monthly* (1872), *The Memorial Story of America* (1892), *The Yosemite Guidebook* (1869), *Harper's Monthly* (1878 & 1879), *Picturesque America* (1872), *Marvels of the New West* (1892), and *Crofutt's Transcontinental Tourist's Guide* (1872).

William R. Jones
former Chief Park Naturalist
Yosemite National Park

GENERAL VIEW OF YOSEMITE,
FROM SUMMIT OF CLOUD'S REST.

ISBN 0-89646-061-4

DESCENT FROM INSPIRATION POINT.
(From Painting by THOMAS HILL.)

CATHEDRAL ROCK.

Tuolumne Big Tree Grove, right across the park to the summit of the range by way of Lake Tenaya, the Big Tuolumne Meadows, and Mount Dana. These roads, with many trails that radiate from Yosemite Valley, bring most of the park within reach of everybody, well or half well.

The three main natural divisions of the park, the lower, middle, and alpine regions, are fairly well defined in altitude, topographical features, and vegetation. The lower, with an average elevation of about five thousand feet, is the region of the great forests, made up of sugar pine, the largest and most beautiful of all the pines in the world; the silvery yellow pine, the next in rank; Douglas spruce, libocedrus, the white and red silver firs, and the *Sequoia gigantea*, or "big tree," the king of conifers, the noblest of a noble race. On warm slopes next the foothills there are a few sabine nut pines; oaks make beautiful groves in the cañon valleys; and poplar, alder, maple, laurel, and Nuttall's flowering dogwood shade the banks of the streams. Many of the pines are more than two hundred feet high, but they are not crowded together. The sunbeams streaming through their feathery arches brighten the ground, and you walk beneath the lofty radiant ceiling in devout subdued mood, as if you were in a grand cathedral with mellow light sifting through colored windows, while the flowery pillared aisles open enchanting vistas in every direction. Scarcely a peak or ridge in the whole region rises bare above the forests, though they are thinly planted in some places where the soil is shallow. From the cool breezy heights you look abroad over a boundless waving sea of evergreens, covering hill and ridge and smooth-flowing slope as far as the eye can reach, and filling every hollow and down-plunging ravine in glorious triumphant exuberance.

Perhaps the best general view of the pine forests of the park, and one of the best in the range, is obtained from the top of the Merced and Tuolumne divide near Hazel Green. On the long, smooth, finely folded slopes of the main ridge, at a height of five to six thousand feet above the sea, they reach most perfect development, and are marshaled to view in magnificent towering ranks, their colossal spires and domes and broad palmlike crowns, deep in the kind sky, rising above one another, — a multitude of giants in perfect health and beauty, — sun-fed mountaineers rejoicing in their strength, chanting with the winds, in accord with the falling waters. The ground is mostly open and inviting to walkers. The fragrant chamæbatia is outspread in rich carpets miles in extent; the manzanita, in orchard-like groves, covered with pink bell-shaped flowers in the spring, grows in openings facing the sun, hazel and buckthorn in the dells; warm brows are purple with mint, yellow with sunflowers and violets; and tall lilies ring their bells around the borders of meadows and along the ferny mossy banks of the streams. Never was mountain forest more lavishly furnished.

Hazel Green is a good place quietly to camp and study, to get acquainted with the trees and birds, to drink the pure water and weather, and to watch the changing lights of the big charmed days. The rose light of the dawn creeping higher among the stars changes to daffodil yellow; then come the level enthusiastic sunbeams pouring across the feathery ridges, touching pine after pine, spruce and fir, libocedrus and lordly sequoia, — searching every recess, until all are awakened and warmed. In the white noon they shine in silvery splendor, every needle and cell in bole and branch thrilling and tingling with ardent life; and the whole landscape glows with consciousness, like the face of a god. The hours go by uncounted. The evening flames with purple and gold. The breeze that has been blowing from the lowlands dies away; and far and near the mighty host of trees baptized in the purple flood stand hushed and thoughtful, awaiting the sun's blessing and farewell, — as impressive a ceremony as if it were never to rise again. When the daylight fades, the night breeze from the snowy summits begins to blow, and the trees, waving and rustling beneath the stars, breathe free again.

It is hard to leave such camps and woods; nevertheless, to the large majority of travelers the middle region of the park is still more interesting, for it has the most striking features of all the Sierra scenery, — the deepest sections of the famous cañons, of which the Yosemite Valley, Hetch-Hetchy Valley, and many smaller ones are wider portions, with level parklike floors and walls of immense height and grandeur of sculpture. This middle region holds also the greater number of the beautiful glacier lakes and glacier meadows, the great granite domes, and the most brilliant and most extensive of the glacier pavements. And though in large part it is severely rocky and bare, it is still rich in trees. The magnificent silver fir (*Abies magnifica*), which ranks with the giants, forms a continuous belt across the park above the pines at an elevation of from seven to nine thousand feet, and north and south of the park boundaries to the extremities of the range, only slightly interrupted by the main cañons. The two-leaved or tamarack pine makes another, less regular belt along the upper margin of the region, while between these two belts, and mingling with them in groves or scattered, are the Patton hemlock, the most graceful of evergreens; the noble mountain pine; the Jeffrey form of the yellow pine, with big cones and long needles; and the brown, burly, sturdy Western juniper. All these except the juniper, which grows on bald rocks, have plenty of flowery brush about them, and gardens in open spaces.

Here, too, lies the broad, shining, heavily sculptured region of primeval granite, which best tells the story of the glacial period on the Pacific side of the continent. No other mountain chain on the globe, as far as I know, is so rich as the Sierra in bold, striking, well-preserved glacial monuments, easily understood by anybody capable of patient observation. Every feature is more or less glacial, and this park portion of the range is the brightest and clearest of all. Not a peak, ridge, dome, cañon, lake basin, garden, forest, or stream but in some way explains the past existence and modes of action of flowing, grinding, sculpturing, soil-making, scenery-making ice. For, notwithstanding the postglacial agents — air, rain, frost, rivers, earthquakes, avalanches — have been at work upon the greater part of the range for tens of thousands of stormy years, engraving their own characters over those of the ice, the latter are so heavily emphasized and enduring that they still rise in sublime relief, clear and legible through every after inscription. The streams have traced only shallow wrinkles as yet, and avalanche, wind, rain, and melting snow have made blurs and scars; but the change effected on the face of the landscape is not greater than is made on the face of a mountaineer by a single year of weathering.

Of all the glacial phenomena presented here, the most striking and attractive to travelers are the polished pavements, because they are so beautiful, and their beauty is of so rare a kind, — unlike any part of the loose earthy lowlands where people dwell and earn their bread. They are simply flat or gently undulating areas of solid resisting granite, the unchanged surface over which the ancient glaciers flowed. They are found in the most perfect condition at an elevation of from eight to nine thousand feet above sea level. Some are miles in extent, only slightly blurred or scarred by spots that have at last yielded to the weather; while the best preserved portions are brilliantly polished, and reflect the sunbeams as calm water or glass, shining as if rubbed and burnished every day, notwithstanding they have been exposed to plashing corroding rains, dew, frost, and melting sloppy snow for thousands of years.

The attention of hunters and prospectors, who see so much in their wild journeys, is seldom attracted by moraines, however regular and artificial-looking; or rocks, however boldly sculptured; or cañons, however deep and sheer-walled. But when they come to these pavements, they go down on their knees and rub their hands admiringly on the glistening surface, and try hard to account for its mysterious smoothness and brightness. They may have seen the winter avalanches come down the mountains, through the woods, sweeping away the trees and scouring the ground; but they conclude that this cannot be the work of avalanches, because the striæ show that the agent, whatever it was, flowed along and around and over the top of high ridges and domes, and also filled the deep cañons. Neither can they see how water could be the agent, for the strange polish is found thousands of feet above the reach of any conceivable flood. Only the winds seem capable of moving over the face of

Yo Semite Falls

the country in the directions indicated by the lines and grooves.

The pavements are particularly fine around Lake Tenaya, and have suggested the Indian name Py-we-ack, the Lake of the Shining Rocks. Indians seldom trouble themselves with geological questions, but a Mono Indian once came to me and asked if I could tell him what made the rocks so smooth at Tenaya. Even dogs and horses, on their first journeys into this region, study geology to the extent of gazing wonderingly at the strange brightness of the ground, and pawing it and smelling it, as if afraid of falling or sinking.

In the production of this admirable hard finish, the glaciers in many places exerted a pressure of more than a hundred tons to the square foot, planing down granite, slate, and quartz alike, showing their structure, and making beautiful mosaics where large feldspar crystals form the greater part of the rock. On such pavements the sunshine is at times dazzling, as if the surface were of burnished silver.

Here, also, are the brightest of the Sierra landscapes in general. The regions lying at the same elevation to the north and south were perhaps subjected to as long and intense a glaciation, but because the rocks are less resisting their polished surfaces have mostly given way to the weather, leaving here and there only small imperfect patches on the most enduring portions of cañon walls protected from the action of rain and snow, and on hard bosses kept comparatively dry by boulders. The short steeply inclined cañons of the east flank of the range are in some places brightly polished, but they are far less magnificent than those of the broad west flank.

One of the best general views of the middle region of the park is to be had from the top of a majestic dome which long ago I named the Glacier Monument. It is situated a few miles to the north of Cathedral Peak, and rises to a height of about fifteen hundred feet above its base and ten thousand above the sea. At first sight it seems sternly inaccessible, but a good climber will find that it may be scaled on the south side. Approaching it from this side you pass through a dense bryanthus-fringed grove of Patton hemlock, catching glimpses now and then of the colossal dome towering to an immense height above the dark evergreens; and when at last you have made your way across woods, wading through azalea and ledum thickets, you step abruptly out of the tree shadows and mossy leafy softness upon a bare porphyry pavement, and behold the dome unveiled in all its grandeur. Fancy a nicely proportioned monument, eight or ten feet high, hewn from one stone, standing in a pleasure ground; magnify it to a height of fif-

Cathedral Peak. Glacier Monument (Fairview Dome).

GLACIER-POLISHED ROCKS. UPPER TUOLUMNE VALLEY.

teen hundred feet, retaining its simplicity of form and fineness, and cover its surface with crystals: then you may gain an idea of the sublimity and beauty of this ice-burnished dome, one of many adorning this wonderful park.

In making the ascent, one finds that the curve of the base rapidly steepens, until one is in danger of slipping; but feldspar crystals, two or three inches long, that have been weathered into relief, afford slight footholds. The summit is in part burnished, like the sides and base, the striæ and scratches indicating that the mighty Tuolumne Glacier, two or three thousand feet deep, overwhelmed it while it stood firm like a boulder at the bottom of a river. The pressure it withstood must have been enormous. Had it been less solidly built, it would have been ground and crushed into moraine fragments, like the general mass of the mountain flank in which at first it lay imbedded; for it is only a hard residual knob or knot with a concentric structure of superior strength, brought into relief by the removal of the less resisting rock about it, — an illustration in stone of the survival of the strongest and most favorably situated.

Hardly less wonderful, when we contemplate the storms it has encountered since first it saw the light, is its present unwasted condition. The whole quantity of postglacial wear and tear it has suffered has not diminished its stature a single inch, as may be readily shown by measuring from the level of the unchanged polished portions of the surface. Indeed, the average postglacial denudation of the entire region, measured in the same way, is found to be less than two inches, — a mighty contrast to that of the ice; for the glacial denudation here has been not less than a mile; that is, in developing the present landscapes, an amount of rock a mile in average thickness has been silently carried away by flowing ice during the last glacial period.

A few erratic boulders nicely poised on the rounded summit of the monument tell an interesting story. They came from a mountain on the crest of the range, about twelve miles to the eastward, floating like chips on the frozen sea, and were stranded here when the top of the monument emerged to the light of day, while the companions of these boulders, whose positions chanced to be over the slopes where they could not find rest, were carried farther on by the shallowing current.

The general view from the summit consists of a sublime assemblage of ice-born mountains and rocks and long wavering ridges, lakes and streams and meadows, moraines in wide-sweeping belts, and beds covered and dotted with forests and groves, — hundreds of square miles of them composed in wild harmony. The snowy mountains on the axis of the range, mostly sharp-peaked and crested, rise in noble array along the sky to the eastward and northward; the gray-pillared Hoffman spur and the Yosemite domes and a countless number of others to the westward; Cathedral Peak with its many spires and companion peaks and domes to the southward; and a smooth billowy multitude of rocks, from fifty feet or less to a thousand feet high, which from their peculiar form seem to be rolling on westward, fill most of the middle ground. Immediately beneath you are the Big Tuolumne Meadows, with an ample swath of dark pine woods on either side, enlivened by the young river, that is seen sparkling and shimmering as it sways from side to side, tracing as best it can its broad glacial channel.

The ancient Tuolumne Glacier, lavishly flooded by many a noble affluent from the snow-laden flanks of Mounts Dana, Gibbs, Lyell, Maclure, and others nameless as yet, poured its majestic overflowing current, four or five miles wide, directly against the high outstanding mass of Mount Hoffman, which divided and

Mount Dana. Glacier-polished surfaces.

CREST OF THE SIERRA, LOOKING EAST.

deflected it right and left, just as a river is divided against an island that stands in the middle of its channel. Two distinct glaciers were thus formed, one of which flowed through the Big Tuolumne Cañon and Hetch-Hetchy Valley, while the other swept upward five hundred feet in a broad current across the divide between the basins of the Tuolumne and Merced into the Tenaya basin, and thence down through the Tenaya Cañon and Yosemite Valley.

The maplike distinctness and freshness of this glacial landscape cannot fail to excite the attention of every observer, no matter how little of its scientific significance he may at first recognize. These bald, glossy, westward-leaning rocks in the open middle ground, with their rounded backs and shoulders toward the glacier fountains of the summit mountains and their split angular fronts looking in the opposite direction, every one of them displaying the form of greatest strength with reference to physical structure and glacial action, show the tremendous force with which through unnumbered centuries the ice flood swept over them, and also the direction of the flow; while the mountains, with their sharp summits and abraded sides, indicate the height to which the glacier rose; and the moraines, curving and swaying in beautiful lines, mark the boundaries of the main trunk and its tributaries as they existed toward the close of the glacial winter. None of the commercial highways of the sea or land, marked with buoys and lamps, fences and guideboards, is so unmistakably indicated as are these channels of the vanished Tuolumne glaciers.

The action of flowing ice, whether in the form of river-like glaciers or broad mantling folds, is but little understood as compared with that of other sculpturing agents. Rivers work openly where people dwell, and so do the rain, and the sea thundering on all the shores of the world; and the universal ocean of air, though unseen, speaks aloud in a thousand voices and explains its modes of working and its power. But glaciers back in their cold solitudes work apart from men, exerting their tremendous energies in silence and darkness. Coming in vapor from the sea, flying invisible on the wind, descending in snow, changing to ice, white, spirit-like, they brood outspread over the predestined landscapes, working on unwearied through unmeasured ages, until in the fullness of time the mountains and valleys are brought forth, channels furrowed for the rivers, basins made for meadows and lakes, and soil beds spread for the forests and fields that man and beast may be fed. Then vanishing like clouds, they melt into streams and go singing back home to the sea.

To an observer upon this adamantine old monument in the midst of such scenery, getting glimpses of the thoughts of God, the day seems endless, the sun stands still. Much faithless fuss is made over the passage in the Bible telling of the standing still of the sun for Joshua. Here you may learn that the miracle occurs for every devout mountaineer, — for everybody doing anything worth doing, seeing anything worth seeing. One day is as a thousand years, a thousand years as one day, and while yet in the flesh you enjoy immortality.

From the monument you will find an easy way down through the woods and along the Big Tuolumne Meadows to Mount Dana, the summit of which commands a grand telling view of the alpine region. The scenery all the way is inspiring, and you saunter on without knowing that you are climbing. The spacious sunny meadows, through the midst of which the bright river glides, extend with but little interruption ten miles to the eastward, dark woods rising on either side to the limit of tree growth, and above the woods a picturesque line of gray peaks and spires dotted with snow banks; while, on the axis of the

Sierra, Mount Dana and his noble compeers repose in massive sublimity, their vast size and simple flowing contours contrasting in the most striking manner with the clustering spires and thin-pinnacled crests crisply outlined on the horizon to the north and south of them.

Tracing the silky lawns, gradually ascending, gazing at the sublime scenery more and more openly unfolded, noting the avalanche gaps in the upper forests, lingering over beds of blue gentians and purple-flowered bryanthus and cassiope, and dwarf willows an inch high in close felted gray carpets, brightened here and there with kalmia and soft creeping mats of vaccinium, sprinkled with pink bells that seem to have been showered down from the sky like hail, — thus beguiled and enchanted, you reach the base of the mountain wholly unconscious of the miles you have walked. And so on to the summit. For all the way up the long red slate slopes that in the distance seemed barren you find little garden beds, and tufts of dwarf phlox, ivesia, and blue arctic daisies that go straight to your heart, blessed fellow mountaineers kept safe and warm by a thousand miracles. You are now more than thirteen thousand feet above the sea, and to the north and south you behold a sublime wilderness of mountains in glorious array, their snowy summits towering together in crowded bewildering abundance, shoulder to shoulder, peak beyond peak. To the east lies the Great Basin, barren-looking and silent, apparently a land of pure desolation, rich only in beautiful light. Mono Lake, fourteen miles long, is outspread below you at a depth of nearly seven thousand feet, its shores of volcanic ashes and sand, treeless and sunburned; a group of volcanic cones, with well-formed, unwasted craters, rises to the south of the lake; while up from its eastern shore innumerable mountains with soft flowing outlines extend range beyond range, gray and pale purple and blue, — the farthest gradually fading on the glowing horizon. Westward you look down and over the countless

"THE YOSEMITE."—[THOMAS HILL.]

moraines, glacier meadows, and grand sea of domes and rock waves of the upper Tuolumne basin, the Cathedral and Hoffman mountains with their wavering lines and zones of forest, the wonderful region to the north of the Tuolumne Cañon, and across the dark belt of silver firs to the pale mountains of the coast.

In the icy fountains of the Mount Lyell and Ritter groups of peaks, to the south of Dana, three of the most important of the Sierra rivers — the Tuolumne, Merced, and San Joaquin — take their rise, their highest tributaries being within a few miles of one another, as they rush forth on their adventurous courses from beneath snow banks and glaciers.

Of the small shrinking glaciers of the Sierra, remnants of the majestic system that sculptured the range, I have seen sixty-five. About twenty-five of them are in the park, and eight are in sight from Mount Dana.

The glacier lakes are sprinkled over all the alpine and subalpine regions, gleaming like eyes beneath heavy rock brows, tree-fringed or bare, embosomed in the woods, and lying in open basins with green and purple meadows around them; but the greater number are in the cool shadowy hollows of the summit mountains not far from the glaciers, the highest lying at an elevation of from eleven to nearly twelve thousand feet above the sea. The whole number in the Sierra, not counting the smallest, can hardly be less than fifteen hundred, of which about two hundred and fifty are in the park. From one standpoint, on Red Mountain, I counted forty-two, most of them within a radius of ten miles. The glacier meadows, which are spread over the filled-up basins of vanished lakes, and form one of the most charming features of the scenery, are still more numerous than the lakes.

An observer stationed here, in the glacial period, would have overlooked a wrinkled mantle of ice as continuous as that which now covers the continent of Greenland; and of all the vast landscape now shining in the sun, he would have seen only the tops of the summit peaks, rising darkly like storm-beaten islands, lifeless and hopeless, above rock-encumbered ice waves. If among the agents that nature has employed in making these mountains there be one that above all others deserves the name of Destroyer, it is the glacier. But we quickly learn that destruction is creation. During the dreary centuries through which the Sierra lay in darkness, crushed beneath the ice folds of the glacial winter, there was a steady invincible advance toward the warm life and beauty of to-day; and it is just where the glaciers crushed most destructively that the greatest amount of beauty is made manifest. But as these landscapes have succeeded the preglacial landscapes, so they in turn are giving place to others already planned and foreseen. The granite domes and pavements, apparently imperishable, we take as symbols of permanence, while these crumbling peaks, down whose frosty gullies avalanches are ever falling, are symbols of change and decay. Yet all alike, fast or slow, are surely vanishing away.

Nature is ever at work building and pulling down, creating and destroying, keeping everything whirling and flowing, allowing no rest but in rhythmical motion, chasing everything in endless song out of one beautiful form into another.

THE FORESTS OF THE YOSEMITE PARK.

THE coniferous forests of the Yosemite Park, and of the Sierra in general, surpass all others of their kind in America, or indeed in the world, not only in the size and beauty of the trees, but in the number of species assembled together, and the grandeur of the mountains they are growing on. Leaving the workaday lowlands, and wandering into the heart of the mountains, we find a new world, and stand beside the majestic pines and firs and sequoias silent and awestricken, as if in the presence of superior beings new arrived from some other star, so calm and bright and godlike they are.

Going to the woods is going home; for I suppose we came from the woods originally. But in some of nature's forests the adventurous traveler seems a feeble, unwelcome creature; wild beasts and the weather trying to kill him, the rank tangled vegetation armed with spears and stinging needles barring his way and making life a hard struggle. Here everything is hospitable and kind, as if planned for your pleasure, ministering to every want of body and soul. Even the storms are friendly and seem to regard you as a brother, their beauty and tremendous fateful earnestness charming alike. But the weather is mostly sunshine, both winter and summer, and the clear sunny brightness of the park is one of its most striking characteristics. Even the heaviest portions of the main forest belt, where the trees are tallest and stand closest, are not in the least gloomy. The sunshine falls in glory through the colossal spires and crowns, each a symbol of health and strength, the noble shafts faithfully upright like the pillars of temples, upholding a roof of infinite leafy interlacing arches and fretted skylights. The more open portions are like spacious parks, carpeted with small shrubs, or only with the fallen needles sprinkled here and there with flowers. In some places, where the ground is level or slopes gently, the trees are assembled in groves, and the flowers and underbrush in trim beds and thickets as in landscape gardens or the lovingly planted grounds of homes; or they are drawn up in orderly rows around meadows and lakes and along the brows of cañons. But in general the forests are distributed in wide belts, in accordance with climate and the comparative strength of each kind in gaining and holding possession of the ground, while anything like monotonous uniformity is prevented by the grandly varied topography, and by the arrangement of the best soil beds in intricate patterns like embroidery; for they are the moraines of ancient glaciers more or less modified by weathering and stream action. These moraines the trees trace over the hills and plateaus and wide furrowed ridges, and far up the sides of the mountains, rising with even growth on levels, and towering above one another on the long rich slopes prepared for them by the vanished glaciers.

Had the Sierra forests been cheaply accessible, the most valuable of them commercially would ere this have fallen a prey to the lumberman. Thus far the redwood of the Coast Mountains and the Douglas spruce of Oregon and Washington have been more available for lumber than the pine of the Sierra. It cost less to go a thousand miles up the coast for timber, where the trees came down to the shores of navigable rivers and bays, than fifty miles up the mountains. Nevertheless, the superior value of the sugar pine for many purposes has tempted capitalists to expend large sums on flumes and railroads to reach the best forests, though perhaps none of these enterprises has paid. Fortunately, the lately established system of parks and reservations has put a stop to any great extension of the business hereabouts, in its most destructive

THE HALF DOME.

forms. And as the Yosemite Park region has escaped the millmen, and the all-devouring hordes of hoofed locusts have been banished, it is still in the main a pure wilderness, unbroken by axe clearings except on the lower margin, where a few settlers have opened spots beside hay meadows for their cabins and gardens. But these are mere dots of cultivation, in no appreciable degree disturbing the grand solitude. Twenty or thirty years ago a good many trees were felled for their seeds; traces of this destructive method of seed-collecting are still visible along the trails; but these as well as the shingle-makers' ruins are being rapidly overgrown, the gardens and beds of underbrush once devastated by sheep are blooming again in all their wild glory, and the park is a paradise that makes even the loss of Eden seem insignificant.

On the way to Yosemite Valley, you get some grand views over the forests of the Merced and Tuolumne basins and glimpses of some of the finest trees by the roadside without leaving your seat in the stage. But to learn how they live and behave in pure wildness, to see them in their varying aspects through the seasons and weather, rejoicing in the great storms, in the spiritual mountain light, putting forth their new leaves and flowers when all the streams are in flood and the birds are singing, and sending away their seeds in the thoughtful Indian summer when all the landscape is glowing in deep calm enthusiasm, like the face of a god, — for this you must love them and live with them, as free from schemes and cares and time as the trees themselves.

And surely nobody will find anything hard in this. Even the blind must enjoy these woods, drinking their fragrance, listening to the music of the winds in their groves, fingering their flowers and plumes and cones and richly furrowed boles. The kind of study required is as easy and natural as breathing. Without any great knowledge of botany or wood-

THE CAP OF LIBERTY AND THE NEVADA FALL.

craft, in a single season you may learn the name and something more of nearly every kind of tree in the park.

With few exceptions all the Sierra trees are growing in the park, — nine species of pine, two of silver fir, and one each of Douglas spruce, libocedrus, hemlock, juniper, and sequoia, — sixteen conifers in all, and about the same number of round-headed trees, oaks, maples, poplars, laurel, alder, dogwood, tumion, etc.

The first of the conifers you meet in going up the range from the west is the digger nut pine (*Pinus sabiniana*), a remarkably open airy wide-branched tree forty to sixty feet high, with long sparse grayish green foliage and large cones. At a height of fifteen to thirty feet from the ground the trunk divides into several main branches, which, after bearing away from one another, shoot straight up and form separate heads as if the axis of the tree had been broken, while the secondary branches divide again and again into rather slender sprays loosely tasseled with leaves eight to twelve inches long. The yellow and purple flowers are about an inch long, the staminate in showy clusters. The big rough burly cones, five to eight or ten inches in length and five or six in diameter, are rich brown in color when ripe, and full of hard-shelled nuts that are greatly prized by Indians and squirrels. This strange-looking pine, enjoying hot sunshine like a palm, is sparsely distributed along the driest part of the Sierra among small oaks and chaparral, and with its gray mist of foliage, strong trunk and branches, and big cones, seen in relief on the glowing sky, forms the most striking feature of the foothill vegetation.

Pinus attenuata is a small slender arrowy tree, with pale green leaves in threes, clustered flowers half an inch long, brownish yellow and crimson, and cones whorled in conspicuous clusters around the branches and also around the trunk. The cones never fall off or open until the tree dies. They are about four inches long, exceedingly strong and solid, and varnished with hard resin forming a waterproof and almost worm and squirrel proof package, in which the seeds are kept fresh and safe during the lifetime of the tree. Sometimes one of the trunk cones is overgrown and imbedded in the heart wood like a knot, but nearly all are pushed out and kept on the surface by the pressure of the successive layers of wood against the base.

This admirable little tree grows on brushy sunbeaten slopes, which from their position and the inflammable character of the vegetation are most frequently fire-swept. These grounds it is able to hold against all comers, however big and strong, by saving its seeds until death, when all it has produced are scattered over the bare cleared ground, and a new generation quickly springs out of the ashes. Thus the curious fact that all the trees of extensive groves and belts are of the same age is accounted for, and their slender habit; for the lavish abundance of seed sown at the same time makes a crowded growth, and the seedlings with an even start rush up in a hurried race for light and life.

Only a few of the attenuata and sabiniana are within the boundaries of the park; the former on the side of the Merced Cañon, the latter on the walls of Hetch-Hetchy Valley and in the cañon below it.

The nut pine (*Pinus monophylla*) is a small, hardy, contented-looking tree, about fifteen or twenty feet high and a foot in diameter. In its youth the close radiating and aspiring branches form a handsome broad-based pyramid, but when fully grown it becomes round-topped, knotty, and irregular, throwing out crooked divergent limbs like an apple tree. The leaves are pale grayish green, about an inch and a half long, and instead of being divided into clusters they are single, round, sharp-pointed, and rigid like spikes, amid which in the spring the red flowers glow brightly.

The cones are only about two inches in length and breadth, but nearly half of their bulk is made up of sweet nuts.

This fruitful little pine grows on the dry east side of the park, along the margin of the Mono sage plain, and is the commonest tree of the short mountain ranges of the Great Basin. Tens of thousands of acres are covered with it, forming bountiful orchards for the red man. Being so low and accessible the cones are easily beaten off with poles, and the nuts procured by roasting until the scales open. To the tribes of the desert and sage plains these seeds are the staff of life. They are eaten either raw or parched, or in the form of mush or cakes after being pounded into meal. The time of nut harvest in the autumn is the Indian's merriest time of all the year. An industrious squirrelish family can gather fifty or sixty bushels in a single month before the snow comes, and then their bread for the winter is sure.

The white pine (*Pinus flexilis*) is widely distributed through the Rocky Mountains and the ranges of the Great Basin, where in many places it grows to a good size, and is an important timber tree where none better is to be found. In the park it is sparsely scattered along the eastern flank of the range from Mono Pass southward, above the nut pine, at an elevation of from eight to ten thousand feet, dwarfing to a tangled bush near the timber-line, but under favorable conditions attaining a height of forty or fifty feet, with a diameter of three to five. The long branches show a tendency to sweep out in bold curves, like those of the mountain and sugar pines, to which it is closely related. The needles are in clusters of five, closely packed on the ends of the branchlets. The cones are about five inches long, — the smaller ones nearly oval, the larger cylindrical. But the most interesting feature of the tree is its bloom, the vivid red pistillate flowers glowing among the leaves like coals of fire.

The dwarf pine or white-barked pine (*Pinus albicaulis*) is sure to interest every observer on account of its curious low matted habit, and the great height on the snowy mountains at which it bravely grows. It forms the extreme edge of the timber-line on both flanks of the summit mountains — if so lowly a tree can be called timber — at an elevation of ten to twelve thousand feet above the sea. Where it is first met on the lower limit of its range it may be twenty or thirty feet high, but farther up the rocky wind-swept slopes, where the snow lies deep and heavy for six months of the year, it makes shaggy clumps and beds, crinkled and pressed flat, over which you can easily walk. Nevertheless in this crushed, down-pressed, felted condition it clings hardily to life, puts forth fresh leaves every spring on the ends of its tasseled branchlets, blooms bravely in the lashing blasts with abundance of gay red and purple flowers, matures its seeds in the short summers, and often outlives the favored giants of the sunlands far below. One of the trees that I examined was only about three feet high, with a stem six inches in diameter at the ground, and branches that spread out horizontally as if they had grown up against a ceiling; yet it was four hundred and twenty-six years old, and one of its supple branchlets, about an eighth of an inch in diameter inside the bark, was seventy-five years old, and so tough that I tied it into knots. At the age of this dwarf many of the sugar and yellow pines and sequoias are seven feet in diameter and over two hundred feet high.

In detached clumps never touched by fire the fallen needles of centuries of growth make fine elastic mattresses for the weary mountaineer, while the tasseled branchlets spread a roof over him, and the dead roots, half resin, usually found in abundance, make capital camp fires, unquenchable in the thickest storms of rain or snow. Seen from a distance the belts and patches darkening the

Top of Half Dome. Cathedral Peak. Vernal Fall. Mount Broderick.

THE CAÑON OF THE MERCED AND THE VERNAL FALL.

mountain sides look like mosses on a roof, and bring to mind Dr. Johnson's remarks on the trees of Scotland. His guide, anxious for the honor of Mull, was still talking of its woods and pointing them out. "Sir," said Johnson, "I saw at Tobermory what they called a wood, which I unluckily took for heath. If you show me what I shall take for furze, it will be something."

The mountain pine (*Pinus monticola*) is far the largest of the Sierra tree mountaineers. Climbing nearly as high as the dwarf albicaulis, it is still a giant in size, bold and strong, standing erect on the storm-beaten peaks and ridges, tossing its cone-laden branches in the rough winds, living a thousand years, and reaching its greatest size — ninety to a hundred feet in height, six to eight in diameter — just where other trees, its companions, are dwarfed. But it is not able to endure burial in snow so long as the albicaulis and flexilis. Therefore, on the upper limit of its range it is found on slopes which, from their steepness or exposure, are least snowy. Its soft graceful beauty in youth, and its leaves, cones, and outsweeping feathery branches, constantly remind you of the sugar pine, to which it is closely allied. An admirable tree, growing nobler in form and size the colder and balder the mountains about it.

The giants of the main forest in the favored middle region are the sequoia, sugar pine, yellow pine, libocedrus, Douglas spruce, and the two silver firs. The park sequoias are restricted to two small groves, a few miles apart, on the Tuolumne and Merced divide, about seventeen miles from Yosemite Valley. The Big Oak Flat road to the valley runs through the Tuolumne Grove, the Coulterville through the Merced. The more famous and better known Mariposa Grove, belonging to the state, lies near the southwest corner of the park, a few miles above Wawona.

The sugar pine (*Pinus Lambertiana*) is first met in the park in open, sunny, flowery woods, at an elevation of about thirty-five hundred feet above the sea, attains full development at a height between five and six thousand feet, and vanishes at the level of eight thousand feet. In many places, especially on the northern slopes of the main ridges between the rivers, it forms the bulk of the forest, but mostly it is intimately associated with its noble companions, above which it towers in glorious majesty on every hill, ridge, and plateau from one extremity of the range to the other, a distance of five hundred miles, — the largest, noblest, and most beautiful of all the seventy or eighty species of pine trees in the world, and of all the coniferous race second only to King Sequoia.

A good many are from two hundred to two hundred and twenty feet in height, with a diameter at four feet from the ground of six to eight feet, and occasionally a grand patriarch, seven or eight hundred years old, is found that is ten or even twelve feet in diameter and two hundred and forty feet high, with a magnificent crown seventy feet wide. David Douglas, who discovered "this most beautiful and immensely grand tree" in the fall of 1826 in southern Oregon, says that the largest of several that had been blown down, "at three feet from the ground was fifty-seven feet nine inches in circumference" (or fully eighteen feet in diameter); "at one hundred and thirty-four feet, seventeen feet five inches; extreme length, two hundred and forty-five feet." Probably for *fifty-seven* we should read *thirty-seven* for the base measurement, which would make it correspond with the other dimensions; for none of this species with anything like so great a girth has since been seen. A girth of even thirty feet is uncommon. A fallen specimen that I measured was nine feet three inches in diameter inside the bark at four feet from the ground, and six feet in diameter at a hundred feet from the ground. A comparatively

CATHEDRAL SPIRES.

young tree, three hundred and thirty years old, that had been cut down, measured seven feet across the stump, was three feet three inches in diameter at a height of one hundred and fifty feet, and two hundred and ten feet in length.

The trunk is a round, delicately tapered shaft, with finely furrowed purplish-brown bark, usually free of limbs for a hundred feet or more. The top is furnished with long and comparatively slender branches, which sweep gracefully downward and outward, feathered with short tasseled branchlets, and divided only at the ends, forming a palmlike crown fifty to seventy-five feet wide, but without the monotonous uniformity of palm crowns or of the spires of most conifers. The old trees are as tellingly varied and picturesque as oaks. No two are alike, and we are tempted to stop and admire every one we come to, whether as it stands silent in the calm balsam-scented sunshine, or waving in accord with enthusiastic storms. The leaves are about three or four inches long, in clusters of five, finely tempered, bright lively green, and radiant. The flowers are but little larger than those of the dwarf pine, and far less showy. The immense cylindrical cones, fifteen to twenty or even twenty-four inches long and three in diameter, hang singly or in clusters, like ornamental tassels, at the ends of the long branches, green, flushed with purple on the sunward side. Like those of almost all the pines they ripen in the autumn of the second season from the flower, and the seeds of all that have escaped the Indians, bears, and squirrels take wing and fly to their places. Then the cones become still more effective as ornaments, for by the spreading of the scales the diameter is nearly doubled, and the color changes to a rich brown. They remain on the tree the following winter and summer; therefore few fertile trees are ever found without them. Nor even after they fall is the beauty work of these grand cones done, for they make a fine show on the flowery, needle-strewn ground. The wood is pale yellow, fine in texture, and deliciously fragrant. The sugar, which gives name to the tree, exudes from the heart wood on wounds made by fire or the axe, and forms irregular crisp white candy-like masses. To the taste of most people it is as good as maple sugar, though it cannot be eaten in large quantities.

No traveler, whether a tree lover or not, will ever forget his first walk in a sugar-pine forest. The majestic crowns approaching one another make a glorious canopy, through the feathery arches of which the sunbeams pour, silvering the needles and gilding the stately columns and the ground into a scene of enchantment.

The yellow pine (*Pinus ponderosa*) is surpassed in size and nobleness of port only by its kingly companion. Full-grown trees in the main forest, where it is associated with the sugar pine, are about one hundred and seventy-five feet high, with a diameter of five to six feet, though much larger specimens may easily be found. The largest I ever measured was a little over eight feet in diameter four feet above the ground, and two hundred and twenty feet high. Where there is plenty of sunshine and other conditions are favorable, it is a massive symmetrical spire, formed of a strong straight shaft clad with innumerable branches, which are divided again and again into stout branchlets laden with bright shining needles and green or purple cones. Where the growth is at all close half or more of the trunk is branchless. The species attains its greatest size and most majestic form in open groves on the deep well-drained soil of lake basins at an elevation of about four thousand feet. There nearly all the old trees are over two hundred feet high, and the heavy, leafy, much-divided branches sumptuously clothe the trunk almost to the ground. Such trees are easily climbed, and in going up the winding stairs of knotty limbs to the top you will gain a most telling and memorable idea of the height, the richness and intricacy of the branches, and the marvelous abundance and beauty of the long shining elastic foliage. In tranquil weather, you will see the firm outstanding needles in calm content, shimmering and throwing off keen minute rays of light like lances of ice; but when heavy winds are blowing, the strong towers bend and wave in the blast with eager wide-awake enthusiasm, and every tree in the grove glows and flashes in one mass of white sunfire.

Both the yellow and sugar pines grow rapidly on good soil where they are not crowded. At the age of a hundred years they are about two feet in diameter and a hundred feet or more high. They are then very handsome, though very unlike: the sugar pine, lithe, feathery, closely clad with ascending branches; the yellow, open, showing its axis from the ground to the top, its whorled branches but little divided as yet, spreading and turning up at the ends with magnificent tassels of long stout bright needles, the terminal shoot with its leaves being often three or four feet long and a foot and a half wide, the most hopeful-looking and the handsomest treetop in the woods. But instead of increasing, like its companion, in wildness and individuality of form with age, it becomes more evenly and compactly spiry. The bark is usually very thick, four to six inches at the ground, and arranged in large plates, some of them on the lower part of the trunk four or five feet long and twelve to eighteen inches wide, forming a strong defense against fire. The leaves are in threes, and from three inches to a foot long. The flowers appear in May: the staminate pink or brown, in conspicuous clusters two or three inches wide; the pistillate crimson, a fourth of an inch wide, and mostly hidden among the leaves on the tips of the branchlets. The cones vary from about three to ten inches in length, two to five in width, and grow in sessile outstanding clusters near the ends of the upturned branchlets.

Being able to endure fire and hunger and many climates this grand tree is widely distributed: eastward from the coast across the broad Rocky Mountain ranges to the Black Hills of Dakota, a distance of more than a thousand miles, and southward from British Columbia near latitude 51° to Mexico, about fifteen hundred miles. South of the Columbia River it meets the sugar pine, and accompanies it all the way down along the Coast and Cascade mountains and the Sierra and southern ranges to the mountains of the peninsula of Lower California, where mountain and tree find their southmost homes together. Pinus ponderosa is extremely variable, and much bother it gives botanists who try to catch and confine the unmanageable proteus in two or a dozen species, — *Jeffreyi*, *deflexa*, *Apacheca latifolia*, etc. But in all its wanderings, in every form it manifests noble strength. Clad in thick bark like a warrior in mail, it extends its bright ranks over all the high ranges of the wild side of the continent: flourishes in the drenching fog and rain of the northern coast at the level of the sea; in the snow-laden blasts of the mountains, and the white glaring sunshine of the interior plateaus and plains; on the borders of mirage-haunted deserts, volcanoes, and lava beds, waving its bright plumes in the hot winds undaunted, blooming every year for centuries, and tossing big ripe cones among the cinders and ashes of nature's hearths.

The Douglas spruce grows with the great pines, especially on the cool north sides of ridges and cañons, and is here nearly as large as the yellow pine, but less abundant. The wood is strong and tough, the bark thick and deeply furrowed, and on vigorous quick-growing trees the stout spreading branches are covered with innumerable slender swaying sprays handsomely clothed with short

MIRROR LAKE.

leaves. The flowers are about three fourths of an inch in length, red or greenish, not so showy as the pendulous bracted cones. But in June and July, when the young bright yellow leaves appear, the entire tree seems to be covered with bloom.

It is this grand tree that forms the famous forests of western Oregon, Washington, and the adjacent coast regions of British Columbia, where it attains its greatest size and is most abundant, making almost pure forests over thousands of square miles, dark and close and almost inaccessible, many of the trees towering with straight imperceptibly tapered shafts to a height of three hundred feet, their heads together shutting out the light, — one of the largest, most widely distributed, and most important of all the Western giants.

The incense cedar (*Libocedrus decurrens*), when full-grown, is a magnificent tree, one hundred and twenty to nearly two hundred feet high, five to eight and occasionally twelve feet in diameter, with cinnamon-colored bark and warm yellow-green foliage, and in general appearance like an arbor vitæ. It is distributed through the main forest from an elevation of three to six thousand feet, and in sheltered portions of cañons on the warm sides to seven thousand five hundred. In midwinter, when most trees are asleep, it puts forth its flowers. The pistillate are pale green and inconspicuous; but the staminate are yellow, about one fourth of an inch long, and are produced in myriads, tingeing all the branches with gold, and making the tree as it stands in the snow look like a gigantic goldenrod. Though scattered rather sparsely amongst its companions in the open woods, it is seldom out of sight, and its bright brown shafts and warm masses of plumy foliage make a striking feature of the landscape. While young and growing fast in an open situation no other tree of its size in the park forms so exactly tapered a pyramid. The branches, outspread in flat plumes and beautifully fronded, sweep gracefully downward and outward, except those near the top, which aspire; the lowest droop to the ground, overlapping one another, shedding off rain and snow, and making fine tents for storm-bound mountaineers and birds. In old age it becomes irregular and picturesque, mostly from accidents: running fires, heavy wet snow breaking the branches, lightning shattering the top, compelling it to try to make new summits out of side branches, etc. Still it frequently lives more than a thousand years, invincibly beautiful, and worthy its place beside the Douglas spruce and the great pines.

This unrivaled forest is still further enriched by two majestic silver firs, *Abies magnifica* and *Abies concolor*, bands of which come down from the main fir belt by cool shady ridges and glens. Abies magnifica is the noblest of its race, growing on moraines, at an elevation of seven thousand to eight thousand five hundred feet above the sea, to a height of two hundred or two hundred and fifty feet, and five to seven in diameter; and with these noble dimensions there is a richness and symmetry and perfection of finish not to be found in any other tree in the Sierra. The branches are whorled, in fives mostly, and stand out from the straight red purple bole in level or, on old trees, in drooping collars, every branch regularly pinnated like fern fronds, and clad with silvery needles, making broad plumes singularly rich and sumptuous.

The flowers are in their prime about the middle of June: the staminate red, growing on the under side of the branchlets in crowded profusion, giving a rich color to nearly all the tree; the pistillate greenish yellow tinged with pink, standing erect on the upper side of the topmost branches; while the tufts of young leaves, about as brightly colored as those of the Douglas spruce, push out of their fragrant brown buds a few weeks later, making another grand show.

The cones mature in a single season from the flowers. When full-grown they are about six to eight inches long, three or four in diameter, blunt, massive, cylindrical, greenish gray in color, covered with a fine silvery down, and beaded with transparent balsam, very rich and precious-looking, standing erect like casks on the topmost branches. If possible, the inside of the cone is still more beautiful. The scales and bracts are tinged with red, and the seed wings are purple with bright iridescence.

Abies concolor, the white silver fir, grows best about two thousand feet lower than the magnifica. It is nearly as large, but the branches are less regularly pinnated and whorled, the leaves are longer, and instead of standing out around the branchlets or turning up and clasping them they are mostly arranged in two horizontal or ascending rows, and the cones are less than half as large. The bark of the magnifica is reddish purple and closely furrowed, that of the concolor is gray and widely furrowed, — a noble pair, rivaled only by the *Abies grandis*, *amabilis*, and *nobilis*, of the forests of Oregon, Washington, and the Northern California Coast Range. But none of these northern species form pure forests that in extent and beauty approach those of the Sierra.

The seeds of the conifers are curiously formed and colored, white, brown, purple, plain or spotted like birds' eggs, and excepting the juniper they are all handsomely and ingeniously winged with reference to their distribution. They are a sort of cunningly devised flying machines, — one-winged birds, birds with but one feather, — and they take but one flight, all save those which, after flying from the cone nest in calm weather, chance to alight on branches where they have to wait for a wind. And though these seed wings are intended for only a moment's use, they are as thoughtfully colored and fashioned as the wings of birds, and require from one to two seasons to grow. Those of the pine, fir, hemlock, and spruce are curved in such manner that, in being dragged through the air by the seeds, they are made to revolve, whirling the seeds in a close spiral, and sustaining them long enough to allow the winds to carry them to considerable distances, — a style of flying full of quick merry motion, strikingly contrasted to the sober dignified sailing of seeds on tufts of feathery pappus. Surely no merrier adventurers ever set out to seek their fortunes. Only in the fir woods are large flocks seen; for, unlike the cones of the pine, spruce, hemlock, etc., which let the seeds escape slowly, one or two at a time, by spreading the scales, the fir cones when ripe fall to pieces, and let nearly all go at once in favorable weather. All along Sierra for hundreds of miles, on dry breezy autumn days, the sunny spaces in the woods among the colossal spires are in a whirl with these shining purple-winged wanderers, notwithstanding the harvesting squirrels have been working at the top of their speed for weeks trying to cut off every cone before the seeds were ready to swarm and fly. Sequoia seeds have flat wings, and glint and glance in their flight like a boy's kite. The dispersal of juniper seeds is effected by the plum and cherry plan of hiring birds at the cost of their board, and thus obtaining the use of a pair of extra good wings.

Above the great fir belt, and below the ragged beds and fringes of the dwarf pine, stretch the broad dark forests of *Pinus contorta*, var. *Murrayana*, usually called tamarack pine. On broad fields of moraine material it forms nearly pure forests at an elevation of about eight or nine thousand feet above the sea, where it is a small well-proportioned tree, fifty or sixty feet high and one or two in diameter, with thin gray bark, crooked much-divided straggling branches, short needles in clusters of two, bright yellow and crimson flowers, and small prickly cones. The very largest I ever measured was ninety feet in height, and a little over six feet in diameter four feet above the ground. On moist well-drained soil in sheltered hollows along streamsides it grows tall and slender with ascending branches, making graceful arrowy spires fifty to seventy-five feet high, with stems only five or six inches thick.

The most extensive forest of this pine in the park lies to the north of the Big Tuolumne Meadows, — a famous deer pasture and hunting ground of the Mono Indians. For miles over wide moraine beds there is an even, nearly pure growth, broken only by glacier meadows, around which the trees stand in trim array, their sharp spires showing to fine advantage both in green flowery summer and white winter. On account of the closeness of its growth in many places, and the thinness and gumminess of its bark, it is easily killed by running fires, which work widespread destruction in its ranks; but a new generation rises quickly from the ashes, for all or a part of its seeds are held in reserve for a year or two or many years, and when the tree is killed the cones open and the seeds are scattered over the burned ground like those of the attenuata.

Next to the mountain hemlock and the dwarf pine this species best endures burial in heavy snow, while in braving hunger and cold on rocky ridgetops it is not surpassed by any. It is distributed from Alaska to Southern California, and inland across the Rocky Mountains, taking many forms in accordance with demands of climate, soil, rivals, and enemies; growing patiently in bogs and on sand dunes beside the sea where it is pelted with salt scud, on high snowy mountains and down in the throats of extinct volcanoes; springing up with invincible vigor after every devastating fire and extending its conquests farther.

The sturdy storm-enduring red cedar (*Juniperus occidentalis*) delights to dwell on the tops of granite domes and ridges and glacier pavements of the upper pine belt, at an elevation of seven to ten thousand feet, where it can get plenty of sunshine and snow and elbowroom without encountering quick-growing overshadowing rivals. They never make anything like a forest, seldom come together even in groves, but stand out separate and independent in the wind, clinging by slight joints to the rock, living chiefly on snow and thin air, and maintaining tough health on this diet for two thousand years or more, every feature and gesture expressing steadfast dogged endurance. The largest are usually about six or eight feet in diameter and fifteen or twenty in height. A very few are ten feet in diameter, and on isolated moraine heaps forty to sixty feet in height. Many are mere stumps, as broad as high, broken by avalanches and lightning, picturesquely tufted with dense gray scalelike foliage, and giving no hint of dying. The staminate flowers are like those of the libocedrus, but smaller; the pistillate are inconspicuous. The wood is red, fine-grained, and fragrant; the bark bright cinnamon and red, and in thrifty trees is strikingly braided and reticulated, flaking off in thin lustrous ribbons, which the Indians used to weave into matting and coarse cloth. These brown unshakable pillars, standing solitary on polished pavements with bossy masses of foliage in their arms, are exceedingly picturesque, and never fail to catch the eye of the artist. They seem sole survivors of some ancient race, wholly unacquainted with their neighbors.

I have spent a good deal of time trying to determine their age, but on account of dry rot, which honeycombs most of the old ones, I never got a complete count of the largest. Some are undoubtedly more than two thousand years old; for though on good moraine soil they grow about as fast as oaks, on bare pavements and smoothly glaciated overswept granite ridges in the dome region they grow extremely slowly. One on the Starr King ridge, only two feet eleven inches in diameter, was eleven hundred and forty years old. Another on the same ridge, only one foot seven and a half inches in diameter, had reached the age of eight hundred and thirty-four years. The first fifteen inches from the bark of a medium-sized tree — six feet in diameter — on the north Tenaya pavement had eight hundred and fifty-nine layers of wood, or fifty-seven to the inch. Beyond this the count was stopped by dry rot and scars of old wounds. The largest I examined was thirty-three feet in girth, or nearly ten in diameter; and though I failed to get anything like a complete count, I learned enough from this and many other specimens to convince me that most of the trees eight to ten feet thick standing on polished glacier pavements are more than twenty centuries of age rather than less. Barring accidents, for all I can see, they would live forever. When killed, they waste out of existence about as slowly as granite. Even when overthrown by avalanches, after standing so long, they refuse to lie at rest, leaning stubbornly on their big elbows as if anxious to rise, and while a single root holds to the rock putting forth fresh leaves with a grim never-say-die and never-lie-down expression.

As the juniper is the most stubborn and unshakable of trees, the mountain hemlock (*Tsuga Mertensiana*) is the most graceful and pliant and sensitive, responding to the slightest touches of the wind. Until it reaches a height of fifty or sixty feet it is sumptuously clothed down to the ground with drooping branches, which are divided into countless delicate waving sprays, grouped and arranged in most indescribably beautiful ways, and profusely sprinkled with handsome brown cones. The flowers also are peculiarly beautiful and effective: the pistillate very dark rich purple; the staminate blue of so fine and pure a tone that the best azure of the high sky seems to be condensed in them.

Though apparently the most delicate and feminine of all the mountain trees, it grows best where the snow lies deepest, at an elevation of from nine thousand to nine thousand five hundred feet, in hollows on the northern slopes of mountains and ridges. But under all circumstances and conditions of weather and soil, sheltered from the main currents of the winds or in blank exposure to them, well fed or starved, it is always singularly graceful in habit. Even at its highest limit in the park, ten thousand five hundred feet above the sea on exposed ridgetops, where it crouches and huddles close together in dwarf thickets like those of the dwarf pine, it still contrives to put forth its sprays and branches in forms of irrepressible beauty, while on moist well-drained moraines it displays a perfectly tropical luxuriance of foliage and flowers and fruits.

In the first winter storms the snow is oftentimes soft, and lodges in the dense leafy branches, pressing them down against the trunk, and the slender drooping axis bends lower and lower as the load increases, until the top touches the ground and an ornamental arch is made. Then, as storm succeeds storm and snow is heaped on snow, the whole tree is at last buried, not again to see the light or move leaf or limb until set free by the spring thaws in June or July. Not the young saplings only are thus carefully covered and put to sleep in the whitest of white beds for five or six months of the year, but trees thirty and forty feet high. From April to May, when the snow is compacted, you may ride over the prostrate groves without seeing a single branch or leaf of them. In the autumn they are full of merry life, when Clark crows, squirrels, and chipmucks are gathering the abundant crop of seeds and cones, and the deer come to rest beneath the thick concealing branches. The finest grove in the park is near Mount Conness, and the trail from the Tuolumne soda springs to the mountain runs through it. Many of the trees in this grove are three to four or five feet in diameter and about a hundred feet high.

The mountain hemlock is widely distributed from near the south extremity of the high Sierra northward along the Cascade Mountains of Oregon and Washington and the coast ranges of British Columbia to Alaska, where it was first discovered in 1827. Its northmost limit, so far as I have observed, is in the icy fiords of Prince William's Sound in latitude 61°, where it forms pure forests at the level of the sea, growing tall and majestic on the banks of the great glaciers, waving in accord with the mountain winds and the thunder of the falling icebergs. Here as in the Sierra it is ineffably beautiful, the very loveliest evergreen in America.

Of the round-headed dicotyledonous trees in the park the most influential are the black and goldcup oaks. They occur in some parts of the main forest belt, scattered among the big pines like a heavier chaparral, but form extensive groves and reach perfect development only in the Yosemite valleys and flats of the main cañons. The California black oak (*Quercus Californica*) is one of the largest and most beautiful of the Western oaks, attaining under favorable conditions a height of sixty to a hundred feet, with a trunk three to seven feet in diameter, wide-spreading picturesque branches, and smooth lively green foliage handsomely scalloped, purple in the spring, yellow and red in autumn. It grows best in sunny open groves, on ground covered with ferns, chokecherry, brier rose, rubus, mints, goldenrods, etc. Few, if any, of the famous oak groves of Europe, however extensive, surpass these in the size and strength and bright airy beauty of the trees, the color and fragrance of the vegetation beneath them, the quality of the light that fills their leafy arches, and in the grandeur of the surrounding scenery. The finest grove in the park is in one of the little Yosemite valleys of the Tuolumne Cañon, a few miles above Hetch-Hetchy.

The mountain live oak, or goldcup oak (*Quercus chrysolepis*), forms extensive groves on earthquake and avalanche taluses and terraces in cañons and Yosemite valleys, from about three to five thousand feet above the sea. In tough, sturdy, unwedgeable strength this is the oak of oaks. In general appearance it resembles the great live oak of the Southern states. It has pale gray bark, a short, uneven, heavily buttressed trunk which divides a few feet above the ground into strong wide-reaching limbs, forming noble arches, and ending in an intricate maze of small branches and sprays, the outer ones frequently drooping in long tresses to the ground like those of the weeping willow, covered with small simple polished leaves, making a canopy broad and bossy, on which the sunshine falls in glorious brightness. The acorn cups are shallow, thick-walled, and covered with yellow fuzzy dust. The flowers appear in May and June with a profusion of pollened tresses, followed by the bronze-colored young leaves.

No tree in the park is a better measure of altitude. In cañons, at an elevation of four thousand feet, you may easily find a tree six or eight feet in diameter; and at the head of a side cañon, three thousand feet higher, up which you can climb in less than two hours, you find the knotty giant dwarfed to a slender shrub, with leaves like those of huckleberry bushes, still bearing acorns, and seemingly contented, forming dense patches of chaparral, on the top of which you may make your bed and sleep softly like a Highlander in heather. About a thousand feet higher it is still smaller, making fringes about a foot high around boulders and along seams in pavements and the brows of cañons, giving handholds here and there on cliffs hard to climb. The largest I have measured were from twenty-five to twenty-seven feet in girth, fifty to sixty feet high, and the spread of the limbs was about double the height. Of all the fifty species of American oaks north of Mexico, as far as I know, only two — the white oak of the Sacramento and San Joaquin valleys, and the live oak of Florida — surpass the mountain live oak in size, while in beauty and calm strength it is not surpassed by any.

The principal riverside trees are poplar, alder, willow, broad-leaved maple, and Nuttall's flowering dogwood. The poplar (*Populus trichocarpa*), often called balm of Gilead from the gum on its buds, is a tall stately tree, towering above its companions as they rise about its strong gray bole, gracefully embowering the banks of the main streams at an elevation of about four thousand feet. Its abundant foliage turns bright yellow in the fall, and the Indian-summer sunshine sifts through it in delightful tones over the slow-gliding waters when they are at their lowest ebb.

The flowering dogwood is brighter still in these calm brooding days, for every branch of its broad head is then a brilliant crimson flame. In the spring, when the streams are in flood, it is the whitest of trees, white as a snowbank with its magnificent flowers four to eight inches in width, making a wonderful show, and drawing swarms of moths and butterflies.

The broad-leaved maple is usually found in the coolest boulder-choked cañons, where the streams are gray and white with foam, over which it spreads its branches in beautiful arches from bank to bank, forming leafy tunnels full of soft green light and spray, — favorite homes of the water ousel. Around the glacier lakes, two or three thousand feet higher, the common aspen grows in fringing lines and groves which are brilliantly colored in autumn, reminding you of the color glory of the Eastern woods.

Scattered here and there or in groves the botanist will find a few other trees, mostly small, — the mountain mahogany, cherry, chestnut, oak, laurel, and nutmeg. The California nutmeg (*Tumion Californicum*) is a handsome evergreen, belonging to the yew family, with pale bark, prickly leaves, fruit like a greengage plum, and seed like a nutmeg. One of the best groves of it in the park is at the Cascades below Yosemite.

But the noble oaks and all these rock-shading, stream-embowering trees are as nothing amid the vast abounding billowy forests of conifers. During my first years in the Sierra I was ever calling on everybody within reach to admire them, but I found no one half warm enough until Emerson came. I had read his essays, and felt sure that of all men he would best interpret the sayings of these noble mountains and trees. Nor was my faith weakened when I met him in Yosemite. He seemed as serene as a sequoia, his head in the empyrean; and forgetting his age, plans, duties, ties of every sort, I proposed an immeasurable camping trip back in the heart of the mountains. He seemed anxious to go, but considerately mentioned his party. I said: "Never mind. The mountains are calling; run away, and let plans and parties and dragging lowland duties all 'gang tapsal-teerie.' We 'll go up a cañon singing your own song, 'Good-by, proud world! I 'm going home,' in divine earnest. Up there lies a new heaven and a new earth; let us go to the show." But alas, it was too late, — too near the sundown of his life. The shadows were growing long, and he leaned on his friends. His party, full of indoor philosophy, failed to see the natural beauty and fullness of promise of my wild plan, and laughed at it in good-natured ignorance, as if it were necessarily amusing to imagine that Boston people might be led to accept Sierra manifestations of God at the price of rough camping. Anyhow, they would have none of it, and held Mr. Emerson to the hotels and trails.

After spending only five tourist days in Yosemite he was led away, but I saw him two days more; for I was kindly invited to go with the party as far as the Mariposa big trees. I told Mr. Emerson that I would gladly go to the sequoias with him, if he would camp in the grove. He consented heartily, and I felt sure that we would have at least one good wild memorable night round a sequoia camp fire. Next day we rode through the magnificent forests of the Merced basin, and I kept calling his attention to the sugar pines, quoting his wood-notes, "Come listen what the pine tree saith," etc., pointing out the noblest as kings and high priests, the most eloquent and commanding preachers of all the mountain forests, stretching forth their century-old arms in benediction over the worshiping congregations crowded about them. He gazed in devout admiration, saying but little, while his fine smile faded away.

Early in the afternoon, when we reached Clark's Station, I was surprised to see the party dismount. And when I asked if we were not going up into the grove to camp they said: "No; it would never do to lie out in the night air. Mr. Emerson might take cold; and you know, Mr. Muir, that would be a dreadful thing." In vain I urged that only in homes and hotels were colds caught, that nobody ever was known to take cold camping in these woods, that there was not a single cough or sneeze in all the Sierra. Then I pictured the big climate-changing, inspiring fire I would make, praised the beauty and fragrance of sequoia flame, told how the great trees would stand about us transfigured in the purple light, while the stars looked down between the great domes; ending by urging them to come on and make an immortal Emerson night of it. But the house habit was not to be overcome, nor the strange dread of pure night air,

Valley Floor, with View of Cathedral Spires.

though it is only cooled day air with a little pure dew in it. So the carpet dust and unknowable reeks were preferred. And to think of this being a Boston choice! Sad commentary on culture and the glorious transcendentalism.

Accustomed to reach whatever place I started for, I was going up the mountain alone to camp, and wait the coming of the party next day. But since Emerson was so soon to vanish, I concluded to stop with him. He hardly spoke a word all the evening, yet it was a great pleasure simply to be near him, warming in the light of his face as at a fire. In the morning we rode up the trail through a noble forest of pine and fir into the famous Mariposa Grove, and stayed an hour or two, mostly in ordinary tourist fashion, — looking at the biggest giants, measuring them with a tape line, riding through prostrate fire-bored trunks, etc., though Mr. Emerson was alone occasionally, sauntering about as if under a spell. As we walked through a fine group, he quoted, "There were giants in those days," recognizing the antiquity of the race. To commemorate his visit, Mr. Galen Clark, the guardian of the grove, selected the finest of the unnamed trees and requested him to give it a name. He named it Samoset, after the New England sachem, as the best that occurred to him.

The poor bit of measured time was soon spent, and while the saddles were being adjusted I again urged Emerson to stay. "You are yourself a sequoia," I said. "Stop and get acquainted with your big brethren." But he was past his prime, and was now as a child in the hands of his affectionate but sadly civilized friends, who seemed as full of old-fashioned conformity as of bold intellectual independence. It was the afternoon of the day and the afternoon of his life, and his course was now westward down all the mountains into the sunset. The party mounted and rode away in wondrous contentment, apparently; tracing the trail through ceanothus and dogwood bushes, around the bases of the big trees, up the slope of the sequoia basin, and over the divide. I followed to the edge of the grove. Emerson lingered in the rear of the train, and when he reached the top of the ridge, after all the rest of the party were over and out of sight, he turned his horse, took off his hat, and waved me a last good-by. I felt lonely, so sure had I been that Emerson of all men would be the quickest to see the mountains and sing them. Gazing awhile on the spot where he vanished, I sauntered back into the heart of the grove, made a bed of sequoia plumes and ferns by the side of a stream, gathered a store of firewood, and then walked about until sundown. The birds, robins, thrushes, warblers, etc., that had kept out of sight, came about me, now that all was quiet, and made cheer. After sundown I built a great fire, and as usual had it all to myself. And though lonesome for the first time in these forests, I quickly took heart again, — the trees had not gone to Boston, nor the birds; and as I sat by the fire, Emerson was still with me in spirit, though I never again saw him in the flesh. He sent books and wrote, cheering me on; advised me not to stay too long in solitude. Soon he hoped my guardian angel would intimate that my probation was at a close. Then I was to roll up my herbariums, sketches, and poems (though I never knew I had any poems), and come to his house; and when I tired of him and his humble surroundings, he would show me to better people.

But there remained many a forest to wander through, many a mountain and glacier to cross, before I was to see his Wachusett and Monadnock, Boston and Concord. It was seventeen years after our parting on the Wawona ridge that I stood beside his grave under a pine tree on the hill above Sleepy Hollow. He had gone to higher Sierras, and, as I fancied, was again waving his hand in friendly recognition.

THE WILD GARDENS OF THE YOSEMITE PARK.

WHEN California was wild, it was the floweriest part of the continent. And perhaps it is so still, notwithstanding the lowland flora has in great part vanished before the farmers' flocks and ploughs. So exuberant was the bloom of the main valley of the state, it would still have been extravagantly rich had ninety-nine out of every hundred of its crowded flowers been taken away, — far flowerier than the beautiful prairies of Illinois and Wisconsin, or the savannas of the Southern states. In the early spring it was a smooth, evenly planted sheet of purple and gold, one mass of bloom more than four hundred miles long, with scarce a green leaf in sight.

Still more interesting is the rich and wonderfully varied flora of the mountains. Going up the Sierra across the Yosemite Park to the Summit peaks, thirteen thousand feet high, you find as much variety in the vegetation as in the scenery. Change succeeds change with bewildering rapidity, for in a few days you pass through as many climates and floras, ranged one above another, as you would in walking along the lowlands to the Arctic Ocean.

And to the variety due to climate there is added that caused by the topographical features of the different regions. Again, the vegetation is profoundly varied by the peculiar distribution of the soil and moisture. Broad and deep moraines, ancient and well weathered, are spread over the lower regions, rough and comparatively recent and unweathered moraines over the middle and upper regions, alternating with bare ridges and domes and glacier-polished pavements, the highest in the icy recesses of the peaks, raw and shifting, some of them being still in process of formation, and of course scarcely planted as yet.

Besides these main soil beds there are many others comparatively small, reformations of both glacial and weather soils, sifted, sorted out, and deposited by running water and the wind on gentle slopes and in all sorts of hollows, potholes, valleys, lake basins, etc., — some in dry and breezy situations, others sheltered and kept moist by lakes, streams, and waftings of waterfall spray, making comfortable homes for plants widely varied. In general, glaciers give soil to high and low places almost alike, while water currents are dispensers of special blessings, constantly tending to make the ridges poorer and the valleys richer. Glaciers mingle all kinds of material together, mud particles and boulders fifty feet in diameter: water, whether in oozing currents or passionate torrents, discriminates both in the size and shape of the material it carries. Glacier mud is the finest meal ground for any use in the Park, and its transportation into lakes and as foundations for flowery garden meadows was the first work that the young rivers were called on to do. Bogs occur only in shallow alpine basins where the climate is cool enough for sphagnum, and where the surrounding topographical conditions are such that they are safe, even in the most copious rains and thaws, from the action of flood currents capable of carrying rough gravel and sand, but where the water supply is nevertheless constant. The mosses dying from year to year gradually give rise to those rich spongy peat beds in which so many of our best alpine plants delight to dwell. The strong winds that occasionally sweep the high Sierra play a more important part in the distribution of special soil beds than is at first sight recognized, carrying forward considerable quantities of sand and gravel, flakes of mica, etc., and depositing them in fields and beds beautifully ruffled and embroidered and adapted to the wants of some of the hardiest and handsomest of the alpine shrubs and flowers. The more resisting of the smooth, solid, glacier-polished domes and ridges can hardly be said to have any soil at all, while others beginning to give way to the weather are thinly sprinkled with coarse angular gravel. Some of them are full of crystals, which as the surface of the rock is decomposed are set free, covering the summits and rolling down the sides in minute avalanches, giving rise to zones and beds of crystalline soil. In some instances the various crystals occur only here and there, sprinkled in the gray gravel like daisies in a sod; but in others half or more is made up of crystals, and the glow of the imbedded or loosely strewn gems and their colored gleams and glintings at different times of the day when the sun is shining might well exhilarate the flowers that grow among them, and console them for being

EL CAPITAN AND THE BRIDAL VEIL FALL.

so completely outshone.

These radiant sheets and belts and dome-encircling rings of crystals are the most beautiful of all the Sierra soil beds, while the huge taluses ranged along the walls of the great cañons are the deepest and roughest. Instead of being slowly weathered and accumulated from the cliffs overhead like common taluses, they were all formed suddenly and simultaneously by an earthquake that occurred at least three centuries ago. Though thus hurled into existence at a single effort, they are the least changeable and destructible of all the soil formations in the range. Excepting those which were launched directly into the channels of rivers, scarcely one of their wedged and interlocked boulders has been moved since the day of their creation, and though mostly made up of huge angular blocks of granite, many of them from ten to fifty feet cube, trees and shrubs make out to live and thrive on them, and even delicate herbaceous plants, — draperia, collomia, zauschneria, etc., — soothing their rugged features with gardens and groves. In general views of the Park scarce a hint is given of its floral wealth. Only by patiently, lovingly sauntering about in it will you discover that it is all more or less flowery, the forests as well as the open spaces, and the mountain tops and rugged slopes around the glaciers as well as the sunny meadows.

Even the majestic cañon cliffs, seemingly absolutely flawless for thousands of feet and necessarily doomed to eternal sterility, are cheered with happy flowers on invisible niches and ledges wherever the slightest grip for a root can be found; as if Nature, like an enthusiastic gardener, could not resist the temptation to plant flowers everywhere. On high, dry rocky summits and plateaus, most of the plants are so small they make but little show even when in bloom. But in the opener parts of the main forests, the meadows, stream banks, and the level floors of Yosemite valleys the vegetation is exceedingly rich in flowers, some of the lilies and larkspurs being from eight to ten feet high. And on the upper meadows there are miles of blue gentians and daisies, white and blue violets ; and great breadths of rosy purple heathworts covering rocky moraines with a marvelous abundance of bloom, enlivened by humming birds, butterflies and a host of other insects as beautiful as flowers. In the lower and middle regions, also, many of the most extensive beds of bloom are in great part made by shrubs, — adenostoma, manzanita, ceanothus, chamæbatia, cherry, rose, rubus, spiræa, shad, laurel, azalea, honeysuckle, calycanthus, ribes, philadelphus, and many others, the sunny spaces about them bright and fragrant with mints, lupines, geraniums, lilies, daisies, goldenrods, castilleias, gilias, pentstemons, etc.

Adenostoma fasciculatum is a handsome, hardy, heathlike shrub belonging to the rose family, flourishing on dry ground below the pine belt, and often covering areas of twenty or thirty square miles of rolling sun-beaten hills and dales with a dense, dark green, almost impenetrable chaparral, which in the distance looks like Scotch heather. It is about six to eight feet high, has slender elastic branches, red shreddy bark, needle-shaped leaves, and small white flowers in panicles about a foot long, making glorious sheets of fragrant bloom in the spring. To running fires it offers no resistance, vanishing with the few other flowery shrubs and vines and liliaceous plants that grow with it about as fast as dry grass, leaving nothing but ashes. But with wonderful vigor it rises again and again in fresh beauty from the root, and calls back to its hospitable mansions the multitude of wild animals that had to flee for their lives.

As soon as you enter the pine woods, you meet the charming little *Chamæbatia foliolosa*, one of the handsomest of the Park shrubs, next in fineness and beauty to the heathworts of the alpine regions. Like adenostoma it belongs to the rose family, is from twelve to eighteen inches high, has brown bark, slender branches, white flowers like those of the strawberry, and thrice-pinnate, glandular, yellow-green leaves, finely cut and fernlike, as if unusual pains had been taken in fashioning them. Where there is plenty of sunshine at an elevation of three thousand to six thousand feet, it makes a close continuous growth, leaf touching leaf over hundreds of acres, spreading a handsome mantle beneath the yellow and sugar pines. Here and there a lily rises above it, an arching bunch of tall bromus, and at wide intervals a rosebush or clump of ceanothus or manzanita, but there are no rough weeds mixed with it, — no roughness of any sort.

Perhaps the most widely distributed of all the Park shrubs and of the Sierra in general, certainly the most strikingly characteristic, are the many species of manzanita (*Arctostaphylos*). Though one species, the *Uva-ursa*, or bearberry, — the kinikinic of the Western Indians, — extends around the world, the greater part of them are Californian. They are mostly from four to ten feet high, roundheaded, with innumerable branches, brown or red bark, pale green leaves set on edge, and a rich profusion of small, pink, narrow-throated, urn-shaped flowers like those of arbutus. The branches are knotty, zigzaggy, and about as rigid as bones, and the bark is so thin and smooth, both trunk and branches seem to be naked, looking as if they had been peeled, polished, and painted red. The wood also is red, hard, and heavy.

These grand bushes seldom fail to engage the attention of the traveler and hold it, especially if he has to pass through closely planted fields of them such as grow on moraine slopes at an elevation of about seven thousand feet, and in cañons choked with earthquake boulders; for they make the most uncompromisingly stubborn of all chaparral. Even bears take pains to go around the stoutest patches if possible, and when compelled to force a passage leave tufts of hair and broken branches to mark their way, while less skillful mountaineers under like circumstances sometimes lose most of their clothing and all their temper.

The manzanitas like sunny ground. On warm ridges and sandy flats at the foot of sun-beaten cañon cliffs, some of the tallest specimens have well-defined trunks six inches to a foot or more thick, and stand apart in orchard-like growths which in bloomtime are among the finest garden sights in the Park. The largest I ever saw had a round, slightly fluted trunk nearly four feet in diameter, which at a height of only eighteen inches from the ground dissolved into a wilderness of branches, rising and spreading to a height and width of about twelve feet. In spring every bush over all the mountains is covered with rosy flowers, in autumn with fruit. The red pleasantly acid berries, about the size of peas, are like little apples, and the hungry mountaineer is glad to eat them, though half their bulk is made up of hard seeds. Indians, bears, coyotes, foxes, birds, and other mountain people live on them for months.

Associated with manzanita there are six or seven species of ceanothus, flowery, fragrant, and altogether delightful shrubs, growing in glorious abundance in the forests on sunny or half-shaded ground, up to an elevation of about nine thousand feet above the sea. In the sugar-pine woods the most beautiful species is *C. integerrimus*, often called California lilac, or deer brush. It is five or six feet high, smooth, slender, willowy, with bright foliage and abundance of blue flowers in close showy panicles.

Two species, *prostratus* and *procumbens*, spread handsome blue-flowered mats and rugs on warm ridges beneath the pines, and offer delightful beds to the tired mountaineer. The commonest species, *C. cordulatus*, is mostly restricted to the silver fir belt. It is white-flowered and thorny, and makes extensive thickets of tangled chaparral, far too dense to wade through, and too deep and loose to walk on, though it is pressed flat every winter by ten or fifteen feet of snow.

Above these thorny beds, sometimes mixed with them, a very wild, red-fruited cherry grows in magnificent tangles, fragrant and white as snow when in bloom. The fruit is small and rather bitter, not so good as the black, puckery chokecherry that grows in the cañons, but thrushes, robins, and chipmunks like it. Below the cherry tangles, chinquapin and goldcup oak spread generous mantles of chaparral, and with hazel and ribes thickets in adjacent glens help to clothe and adorn the rocky wilderness, and produce food for the many mouths Nature has to fill. *Azalea occidentalis* is the glory of cool streams and meadows. It is from two to five feet high, has bright green leaves and a rich profusion of large, fragrant white and yellow flowers, which are in prime beauty in June, July, and August, according to the elevation (from three thousand to six thousand feet). Only the purple-flowered rhododendron of the redwood forests rivals or surpasses it in superb abounding bloom.

Back a little way from the azalea-bordered streams, a small wild rose makes thickets, often several acres in extent, deliciously fragrant on dewy mornings and after showers, the fragrance mingled with the music of the birds nesting in them. And not far from these rose gardens, *Rubus Nutkanus* covers the ground with broad velvety leaves and pure white flowers as large as those of its neighbor the rose, and finer in texture; followed at the end of summer by soft red berries good for bird and beast and man also. This is the commonest and the most beautiful of the whole blessed flowery fruity genus.

The glory of the alpine region in

bloomtime are the heathworts, cassiope, bryanthus, kalmia, and vaccinium, enriched here and there by the alpine honeysuckle *Lonicera conjugialis*, and by the purple-flowered *Primula suffruticosa*, the only primrose discovered in California, and the only shrubby species in the genus. The lowly, hardy, adventurous cassiope has exceedingly slender creeping branches, scalelike leaves, and pale pink or white waxen bell flowers. Few plants, large or small, so well endure hard weather and rough ground over so great a range. In July it spreads a wavering, interrupted belt of the loveliest bloom around glacier lakes and meadows and across wild moory expanses, between roaring streams, all along the Sierra, and northward beneath cold skies by way of the mountain chains of Oregon, Washington, British Columbia, and Alaska to the Arctic regions; gradually descending, until at the north end of the continent it reaches the level of the sea; blooming as profusely and at about the same time on mossy frozen tundras as on the high Sierra moraines. Bryanthus, the companion of cassiope, accompanies it as far north as southeastern Alaska, where together they weave thick plushy beds on rounded mountain tops above the glaciers. Bryanthus grows mostly at slightly lower elevations; the upper margin of what may be called the bryanthus belt in the Sierra uniting with and overlapping the lower margin of the cassiope.

The wide bell-shaped flowers are bright purple, about three fourths of an inch in diameter, hundreds to the square yard, the young branches, mostly erect, being covered with them. No Highlander in heather enjoys more luxurious rest than the Sierra mountaineer in a bed of blooming bryanthus. And imagine the show on calm dewy mornings, when there is a radiant globe in the throat of every flower, and smaller gems on the needle-shaped leaves, the sunbeams pouring through them. In the same wild cold region the tiny *Vaccinium myrtillus*, mixed with kalmia and dwarf willows, spreads thinner carpets, the down-pressed matted leaves profusely sprinkled with pink bells; and on higher sandy slopes you will find several alpine species of eriogonum with gorgeous bossy masses of yellow bloom, and the lovely Arctic daisy with many blessed companions; charming plants, gentle mountaineers, Nature's darlings, which seem always the finer the higher and stormier their homes.

Many interesting ferns are distributed over the Park from the foothills to a little above the timber line. The greater number are rock ferns, — pellæa, cheilanthes, polypodium, adiantum, woodsia, cryptogramme, etc., with small tufted fronds, lining glens and gorges and fringing the cliffs and moraines. The most important of the larger species are woodwardia, aspidium, asplenium, and the common pteris. *Woodwardia radicans* is a superb fern five to eight feet high, growing in vaselike clumps where the ground is level, and on slopes in a regular thatch, frond over frond, like shingles on a roof. Its range in the Park is from the western boundary up to about five thousand feet, mostly on benches of the north walls of cañons watered by small outspread streams. It is far more abundant in the Coast Mountains beneath the noble redwoods, where it attains a height of ten to twelve feet. The aspidiums are mostly restricted to the moist parts of the lower forests, *Asplenium filix-fœmina* to marshy streams. The hardy, broad-shouldered *Pteris aquilina*, the commonest of ferns, grows tall and graceful on sunny flats and hillsides, at elevations between three thousand and six thousand feet. Those who know it only in the Eastern states can form no fair conception of its stately beauty in the sunshine of the Sierra. On the level sandy floors of Yosemite valleys it often attains a height of six to eight feet in fields thirty or forty acres in extent, the magnificent fronds outspread in a nearly

BOTANIST'S MOUNTAIN BOQUET

horizontal position, forming a ceiling beneath which one may walk erect in delightful mellow shade. No other fern does so much for the color glory of autumn, with its browns and reds and yellows changing and interblending. Even after lying dead all winter beneath the snow it spreads a lively brown mantle over the desolate ground, until the young fronds with a noble display of faith and hope come rolling up into the light through the midst of the beautiful ruins. A few weeks suffice for their development, then, gracefully poised each in its place, they manage themselves in every exigency of weather as if they had passed through a long course of training. I have seen solemn old sugar pines thrown into momentary confusion by the sudden onset of a storm, tossing their arms excitedly as if scarce awake, and wondering what had happened, but I never noticed surprise or embarrassment in the behavior of this noble pteris. Of five species of pellæa in the Park, the handsome andromedæfolia growing in brushy foothills with *Adiantum emarginatum* is the largest. *P. Breweri*, the hardiest and at the same time the most fragile of the genus, grows in dense tufts among rocks on storm-beaten mountain sides along the upper margin of the fern line. It is a charming little fern four or five inches high, has shining bronze-colored stalks which are about as brittle as glass, and pale green pinnate fronds. Its companions on the lower part of its range are *Cryptogramme acrostichoides* and *Phegopteris alpestis*, the latter soft and tender, not at all like a rock fern, though it grows on rocks where the snow lies longest.

P. Bridgesii, with blue-green, narrow, simply pinnate fronds, is about the same size as Breweri and ranks next to it as a mountaineer, growing in fissures and around boulders on glacier pavements. About a thousand feet lower we find the smaller and more abundant *P. densa*, on ledges and boulder-strewn fissured pavements, watered until late in summer by oozing currents from snow banks or thin outspread streams from moraines, growing in close sods, its little, bright green, triangular, tripinnate fronds, about an inch in length, as innumerable as leaves of grass. *P. ornithopus* has twice or thrice pinnate fronds, is dull in color, and dwells on hot rocky hillsides among chaparral.

Three species of *Cheilanthes*, — *Californica*, *gracillima*, and *myriophylla*, with beautiful two to four pinnate fronds, an inch to five inches long, adorn the stupendous walls of the cañons however dry and sheer. The exceedingly delicate and interesting Californica is rare, the others abundant at from three thousand to seven thousand feet elevation, and are often accompanied by the little gold fern, *Gymnogramme triangularis*, and rarely by the curious little *Botrychium simplex*, the smallest of which are less than an inch high.

The finest of all the rock ferns is *Adiantum pedatum*, lover of waterfalls and the lightest waftings of irised spray. No other Sierra fern is so constant a companion of white spray-covered streams, or tells so well their wild thundering music. The homes it loves best are cave-like hollows beside the main falls, where it can float its plumes on their dewy breath, safely sheltered from the heavy spray-laden blasts. Many of these moss-lined chambers, so cool, so moist, and brightly colored with rainbow light, contain thousands of these happy ferns, clinging to the emerald walls by the slightest holds, reaching out the most wonderfully delicate fingered fronds on dark glossy stalks, sensitive, tremulous, all alive, in an attitude of eager attention; throbbing in unison with every motion and tone of the resounding waters, compliant to their faintest impulses, moving each division of the frond separately at times as if fingering the music, playing on invisible keys.

Considering the lilies as you go up the mountains, the first you come to is *L. pardalinum*, with large orange-yellow, purple-spotted flowers big enough for babies' bonnets. It is seldom found higher than thirty-five hundred feet above the sea, grows in magnificent groups of fifty to a hundred or more, in romantic waterfall dells in the pine woods, shaded by overarching maple and willow, alder and dogwood, with bushes in front of the embowering trees for a border, and ferns and sedges in front of the bushes; while the bed of black humus in which the bulbs are set is carpeted with mosses and liverworts. These richly furnished lily gardens are the pride of the falls on the lower tributaries of the Tuolumne and Merced rivers, falls not like those of Yosemite valleys coming from the sky with rock-shaking thunder tones, but small, with low, kind voices cheerily singing in calm leafy bowers, self-contained, keeping their snowy skirts well about them, yet furnishing plenty of spray for the lilies.

The Washington lily (*L. Washingtonianum*) is white, deliciously fragrant, moderate in size, with three to ten flowered racemes. The largest I ever measured was eight feet high, the raceme two feet long, with fifty-two flowers, fifteen of them open; the others had faded or were still in the bud. This famous lily is distributed over the sunny portions of the sugar-pine woods, never in large garden companies like pardalinum, but widely scattered, standing up to the waist in dense ceanothus and manzanita chaparral, waving its lovely flowers above the blooming wilderness of brush, and giving their fragrance to the breeze. These stony, thorny jungles are about the last places in the mountains in which one would look for lilies. But though they toil not nor spin, like other people under adverse circumstances, they have to do the best they can. Because their large bulbs are good to eat they are dug up by Indians and bears; therefore, like hunted animals, they seek refuge in the cha-

INDIAN SQUAWS GATHERING STRAWBERRIES IN THE VALLEY.

parral, where among the boulders and tough tangled roots they are comparatively safe. This is the favorite Sierra lily, and it is now growing in all the best parks and gardens of the world.

The showiest gardens in the Park lie imbedded in the silver fir forests on the top of the main dividing ridges or hang like gayly colored scarfs down their sides. Their wet places are in great part taken up by veratrum, a robust broad-leaved plant, determined to be seen, and habenaria and spiranthes; the drier parts by tall columbines, larkspurs, castilleias, lupines, hosackias, erigerons, valerian, etc., standing deep in grass, with violets here and there around the borders. But the finest feature of these forest gardens is *Lilium parvum*. It varies greatly in size, the tallest being from six to nine feet high, with splendid racemes of ten to fifty small orange-colored flowers, which rock and wave with great dignity above the other flowers in the infrequent winds that fall over the protecting wall of trees. Though rather frail-looking it is strong, reaching prime vigor and beauty eight thousand feet above the sea, and in some places venturing as high as eleven thousand.

Calochortus, or Mariposa tulip, is a unique genus of many species confined to the California side of the continent; charming plants, somewhat resembling the tulips of Europe, but far finer. The richest calochortus region lies below the western boundary of the Park, still five or six species are included. *C. Nuttallii* is common on moraines in the forests of the two-leaved pine; and *C. cœruleus* and *nudus*, very slender, lowly species, may be found in moist garden spots near Yosemite. *C. albus*, with pure white flowers, growing in shady places among the foothill shrubs, is, I think, the very loveliest of all the lily family, — a spotless soul, plant saint, that every one must love and so be made better. It puts the wildest mountaineer on his good behavior. With this plant the whole world would seem rich though none other existed. Next after Calochortus, Brodiæa is the most interesting genus. Nearly all the many species have beautiful showy heads of blue, lilac, and yellow flowers, enriching the gardens of the lower pine region. Other liliaceous plants likely to attract attention are the blue-flowered camassia, the bulbs of which are prized as food by Indians; fritillaria, smilicina, chloragalum, and the twining climbing stropholirion.

The common orchidaceous plants are corallorhiza, goodyera, spiranthes, and habenaria. *Cypripedium montanum*, the only moccasin flower I have seen in the Park, is a handsome, thoughtful-looking plant living beside cool brooks. The large oval lip is white, delicately veined with purple; the other petals and sepals purple, strap-shaped, and elegantly curved and twisted.

To tourists the most attractive of all the flowers of the forest is the snow plant (*Sarcodes sanguinea*). It is a bright red, fleshy, succulent pillar that pushes up through the dead needles in the pine and fir woods like a gigantic asparagus shoot. The first intimation of its coming is a loosening and upbulging of the brown stratum of decomposed needles on the forest floor in the cracks of which you notice fiery gleams; presently a blunt dome-shaped head an inch or two in diameter appears, covered with closely imbricated scales and bracts. In a week or so it grows to a height of six to twelve inches. Then the long fringed bracts spread and curl aside, allowing the twenty or thirty five-lobed bell-shaped flowers to open and look straight out from the fleshy axis. It is said to grow up through the snow; on the contrary it always waits until the ground is warm, though with other early flowers it is occasionally buried or half buried for a day or two by spring storms. The entire plant — flowers, bracts, stem, scales, and roots — is red. But notwithstanding its glowing color and beautiful flowers, it is singularly unsympathetic and cold. Everybody admires it as a wonderful curiosity, but nobody loves it. Without fragrance, rooted in decaying vegetable matter, it stands beneath the pines and firs lonely, silent, and about as rigid as a graveyard monument.

Down in the main cañons adjoining the azalea and rose gardens there are fine beds of herbaceous plants, — tall mints and sunflowers, iris, œnothera, brodiæa, and bright beds of erythræa on the ferny meadows. Bolandera, sedum, and airy feathery purple-flowered heuchera adorn mossy nooks near falls, the shading trees wreathed and festooned with wild grapevines and clematis; while lightly shaded flats are covered with gilia and eunanus of many species, hosackia, arnica, chænactis, gayophytum, gnaphalium, monardella, etc.

Thousands of the most interesting gardens in the Park are never seen, for they are small and lie far up on ledges and terraces of the sheer cañon walls, wherever a strip of soil however narrow and shallow can rest. The birds, winds, and down-washing rains have planted them with all sorts of hardy mountain flowers, and where there is sufficient moisture they flourish in profusion. Many of them are watered by little streams that seem lost on the tremendous precipices, clinging to the face of the rock in lacelike strips, and dripping from ledge to ledge, too silent to be called falls, pathless wanderers from the upper meadows, which for centuries have been seeking a way down to the rivers they belong to, without having worn as yet any appreciable channel, mostly evaporated or given to the plants they meet before reaching the foot of the cliffs. To these unnoticed streams the finest of the cliff gardens owe their luxuriance and freshness of beauty. In the larger ones ferns and showy flowers flourish in wonderful profusion, — woodwardia, columbine, collomia, castilleia, draperia, geranium, erythræa, pink and scarlet mimulus, hosackia, saxifrage, sunflowers, and daisies, with azalea, spiræa, and calycanthus, a few specimens of each that seem to have been culled from the large gardens above and beneath them. Even lilies are occasionally found in these irrigated cliff gardens, swinging their bells over the giddy precipices, seemingly as happy as their relatives down in the waterfall dells.

Most of the cliff gardens, however, are dependent on summer showers, and though from the shallowness of the soil beds they are often dry, they still display a surprising number of bright flowers, — scarlet zauschneria, purple bush-penstemon, mints, gilias, and bosses of glowing golden bahia. Nor is there any lack of commoner plants; the homely yarrow is often found in them, and sweet clover and honeysuckle for the bees. In the upper cañons, where the walls are inclined at so low an angle that they are loaded with moraine material through which perennial streams percolate in broad diffused currents, there are long wavering garden beds, that seem to be descending through the forest like cascades, their fluent lines suggesting motion, swaying from side to side of the forested banks, surging up here and there over island-like boulder piles, or dividing and flowing around them. In some of these floral cascades the vegetation is chiefly sedges and grasses ruffled with willows; in others, showy flowers like those of the lily gardens on the main divides. Another curious and picturesque series of wall gardens are made by thin streams that ooze slowly from moraines and slip gently over smooth glaciated slopes. From particles of sand and mud they carry, a pair of lobe-shaped sheets of soil an inch or two thick are gradually formed, one of them hanging down from the brow of the slope, the other leaning up from the foot of it like stalactite and stalagmite, the soil being held together by the flowery, moisture-loving plants growing in it.

Along the rocky parts of the cañon bottoms between lake basins, where the streams flow fast over glacier-polished granite, there are rows of pothole gardens full of ferns, daisies, goldenrods, and other common plants of the neighborhood nicely arranged like bouquets, and standing out in telling relief on the bare shining rock banks. And all the way up the cañons to the Summit mountains, wherever there is soil of any sort, there is no lack of flowers, however short the summer may be. Within eight or ten feet of a snowbank, lingering beneath a shadow, you may see belated ferns unrolling their fronds in September, and sedges hurrying up their brown spikes, on ground that has been free from snow only eight or ten days, and is likely to be covered again within a few weeks; the winter in the coolest of these shadow gardens being about eleven months long, while spring, summer, and autumn are hurried and crowded into one month. Again, under favorable conditions, alpine gardens three or four thousand feet higher than the last are in their prime in June. Between the Summit peaks at the head of the cañons surprising effects are produced, where the sunshine falls direct on rocky slopes and reverberates among boulders. Toward the end of August, in one of these natural hothouses on the north shore of a glacier lake 11,500 feet above the sea, I found a luxuriant growth of hairy lupines, thistles, goldenrods, shrubby potentilla, Spraguea, and the mountain epilobium with thousands of purple flowers an inch wide, while the opposite shore, at a distance of only three hundred yards, was bound in heavy avalanche snow, — flowery summer on one side, winter on the other. And I know a bench garden on the north wall of Yosemite in which a few flowers are in bloom all winter; the massive rocks about it storing up sunshine enough in summer to melt the snow about as fast as it falls. When tired of the confinement of my cabin I used to camp out in it in January, and never failed to find flowers, and butterflies also, except during snowstorms and a few days after.

From Yosemite one can easily walk in a day to the top of Mount Hoffman, a massive gray mountain that rises in the centre of the Park, with easy slopes adorned with castellated piles and crests on the south side, rugged precipices banked with perpetual snow on the north. Most of the broad summit is comparatively level and smooth, and covered with crystals of quartz, — mica, hornblende, feldspar, garnet, zircon, tourmaline, etc., weathered out and strewn loosely as if sown broadcast; their radiance so dazzling in some places as fairly to hide the multitude of small flowers that grow among them; myriads of keen lance rays infinitely fine, white or colored, making an almost continuous glow over all the ground, with here and there throbbing, spangling lilies of light growing on the larger gems. At first sight only these crystal sunflowers are noticed, but looking closely you discover minute gilias, ivesias, eunanus, phloxes, etc., in thousands, showing more petals than leaves; and larger plants in hollows and on the borders of rills, — lupines, potentillas, daisies, harebells, mountain columbine, astragalus, fringed with heathworts. You wander about from garden to garden enchanted, as if walking among stars, gathering the brightest gems, each and all apparently doing their best with eager enthusiasm, as if everything depended on faithful shining; and considering the flowers basking in the glorious light, many of them looking like swarms of small moths and butterflies that were resting after long dances in the sunbeams. Now your attention is called to colonies of woodchucks and pikas, the mounds in front of their burrows glittering like heaps of jewelry, — romantic ground to live in or die in. Now you look abroad over the vast round landscape bounded by the down-curving sky, nearly all the Park in it displayed like a map, — forests, meadows, lakes, rock-waves, and snowy mountains. Northward lies the basin of Yosemite Creek, paved with bright domes and lakes like larger crystals; eastward, the meadowy, billowy Tuolumne region and the Summit peaks in glorious array; southward, Yosemite; and westward, the boundless forests. On no other mountain that I know of are you more likely to linger. It is a magnificent camp ground. Clumps of dwarf pine furnish rosiny roots and branches for fuel, and the rills pure water. Around your camp fire the flowers seem to be looking eagerly at the light, and the crystals shine unweariedly, making fine company as you lie at rest in the very heart of the vast, serene, majestic night.

The finest of the glacier meadow gardens lie at an elevation of about nine thousand feet, imbedded in the upper pine forests like lakes of light. They are smooth and level, a mile or two long, and the rich, well-drained ground is completely covered with a soft, silky, plushy sod enameled with flowers, not one of which is in the least weedy or coarse. In some places the sod is so crowded with showy flowers that the grasses are scarce noticed, in others they are rather sparingly scattered; while every leaf and flower seems to have its winged representative in the swarms of happy flower-like insects that enliven the air above them.

With the winter snowstorms wings and petals are folded, and for more than half the year the meadows are snow-buried ten or fifteen feet deep. In June they begin to thaw out, small patches of the dead sloppy sod appear, gradually increasing in size until they are free and warm again, face to face with the sky; myriads of growing points push through the steaming mould, frogs sing cheeringly, soon joined by the birds, and the merry insects come back as if suddenly raised from the dead. Soon the ground is green with mosses and liverworts and dotted with small fungi, making the first crop of the season. Then the grass leaves weave a new sod, and the exceedingly slender panicles rise above it like a purple mist, speedily followed by potentilla, ivesia, bossy orthocarpus yellow and purple, and a few pentstemons. Later come the daisies and goldenrods, asters and gentians. Of the last there are three species, small and fine with varying tones of blue, and in glorious abundance, coloring extensive patches where the sod is shallowest. Through the midst flows a stream only two or three feet wide, silently gliding as if careful not to disturb the hushed calm of the solitude, its banks embossed by the common sod bent down to the water's edge, and trimmed with mosses and violets; slender grass panicles lean over like miniature pine trees, and here and there on the driest places small mats of heathworts are neatly spread, enriching without roughening the bossy down-curling sod. In spring and summer the weather is mostly crisp, exhilarating sunshine, though magnificent mountain ranges of cumuli are often upheaved about noon, their shady hollows tinged with purple ineffably fine, their snowy sun-beaten bosses glowing against the sky, casting cooling shadows for an hour or two, then dissolving in a quick washing rain. But for days in succession there are no clouds at all, or only faint wisps and pencilings scarcely discernible.

Toward the end of August the sunshine grows hazy, announcing the coming of Indian summer, the outlines of the landscapes are softened and mellowed, and more and more plainly are the mountains clothed with light, white tinged with pale purple, richest in the morning and evening. The warm, brooding days are full of life and thoughts of life to come, ripening seeds with next summer in them or a hundred summers. The nights are unspeakably impressive and calm, frost crystals of wondrous beauty grow on the grass, — each carefully planned and finished as if intended to endure forever. The sod becomes yellow and brown, but the late asters and gentians, carefully closing their flowers at night, do not seem to feel the frost; no nipped, wilted plants of any kind are to be seen; even the early snowstorms fail to blight them. At last the precious seeds are ripe, all the work of the season is done, and the sighing pines tell the coming of winter and rest.

Ascending the range you find that many of the higher meadows slope considerably, from the amount of loose material washed into their basins; and sedges and rushes are mixed with the grasses or take their places, though all are still more or less flowery and bordered with heathworts, sibbaldea, and dwarf willows. Here and there you come to small bogs, the wettest smooth and adorned with parnassia and buttercups, others tussocky and ruffled like bits of Arctic tundra, their mosses and lichens interwoven with dwarf shrubs. On boulder piles the red iridescent oxyria abounds, and on sandy, gravelly slopes several species of shrubby, yellow-flowered eriogonum, some of the plants, less than a foot high, being very old, a century or more, as is shown by the rings made by the annual whorls of leaves on the big roots. Above these flower-dotted slopes the gray, savage wilderness of crags and peaks seems lifeless and bare. Yet all the way up to the tops of the highest mountains, commonly supposed to be covered with eternal snow, there are bright garden spots crowded with flowers, their warm colors calling to mind the sparks and jets of fire on polar volcanoes rising above a world of ice. The principal mountain-top plants are phloxes, drabas, saxifrages, silene, cymopterus, hulsea, and polemonium, growing in detached stripes and mats,

— the highest streaks and splashes of the summer wave as it breaks against these wintry heights. The most beautiful are the phloxes (douglasii and cæspitosum), and the red-flowered silene with innumerable flowers hiding the leaves. Though herbaceous plants, like the trees and shrubs, are dwarfed as they ascend, two of these mountain dwellers, *Hulsea algida* and *Polemonium confertum*, are notable exceptions. The yellow-flowered hulsea is eight to twelve inches high, stout, erect, the leaves, three to six inches long, secreting a rosiny, fragrant gum, standing up boldly on the grim lichen-stained crags, and never looking in the least tired or discouraged. Both the ray and disk flowers are yellow, the heads nearly two inches wide, and are eagerly sought for by roving bee mountaineers. The polemonium is quite as luxuriant and tropical-looking as its companion, about the same height, glandular, fragrant, its blue flowers closely packed in eight or ten heads, twenty to forty in a head. It is never far from hulsea, growing at elevations between eleven and thirteen thousand feet wherever a little hollow or crevice favorably situated with a handful of wind-driven soil can be found.

From these frosty Arctic sky gardens you may descend in one straight swoop to the abronia, mentzelia, and œnothera gardens of Mono, where the sunshine is warm enough for palms.

But the greatest of all the gardens is the belt of forest trees, profusely covered in the spring with blue and purple, red and yellow blossoms, each tree with a gigantic panicle of flowers fifty to a hundred feet long. Yet strange to say they are seldom noticed. Few travel through the woods when they are in bloom, the flowers of some of the showiest species opening before the snow is off the ground. Nevertheless, one would think the news of such gigantic flowers would quickly spread, and travelers from all the world would make haste to the show. Eager inquiries are made for the bloomtime of rhododendron-covered mountains and for the bloomtime of Yosemite streams, that they may be enjoyed in their prime; but the far grander outburst of tree bloom covering a thousand mountains — who inquires about that? That the pistillate flowers of the pines and firs should escape the eyes of careless lookers is less to be wondered at, since they mostly grow aloft on the topmost branches, and can hardly be seen from the foot of the trees. Yet even these make a magnificent show from the top of an overlooking ridge when the sunbeams are pouring through them. But the far more numerous staminate flowers of the pines in large rosy clusters, and those of the silver firs in countless thousands on the under side of the branches, cannot be hid, stand where you may. The mountain hemlock also is gloriously colored with a profusion of lovely blue and purple flowers, a spectacle to gods and men. A single pine or hemlock or silver fir in the prime of its beauty about the middle of June is well worth the pains of the longest journey; how much more broad forests of them thousands of miles long.

One of the best ways to see tree flowers is to climb one of the tallest trees and to get into close tingling touch with them, and then look abroad. Speaking of the benefits of tree climbing, Thoreau says: "I found my account in climbing a tree once. It was a tall white pine, on the top of a hill; and though I got well pitched, I was well paid for it, for I discovered new mountains in the horizon which I had never seen before. I might have walked about the foot of the tree for threescore years and ten, and yet I certainly should never have seen them. But, above all, I discovered around me, — it was near the middle of June, — on the ends of the topmost branches, a few minute and delicate red conelike blossoms, the fertile flower of the white pine looking heavenward. I

Humming Birds Glinting among the Flowers.

carried straightway to the village the topmost spire, and showed it to stranger jurymen who walked the streets, — for it was court week, — and to farmers and lumbermen and woodchoppers and hunters, and not one had ever seen the like before, but they wondered as at a star dropped down."

The same marvelous blindness prevails here, although the blossoms are a thousandfold more abundant and telling. Once when I was collecting flowers of the red silver fir near a summer tourist resort on the mountains above Lake Tahoe, I carried a handful of flowery branches to the boarding house, where they quickly attracted a wondering, admiring crowd of men, women, and children. "Oh, where did you get these?" they cried. "How pretty they are — mighty handsome — just too lovely for anything — where do they grow?" "On the commonest trees about you," I replied. "You are now standing beside one of them, and it is in full bloom; look up." And I pointed to a blossom-laden *Abies magnifica*, about a hundred and twenty feet high, in front of the house, used as a hitching post. And seeing its beauty for the first time, their wonder could hardly have been greater or more sincere had their silver fir hitching post blossomed for them at that moment as suddenly as Aaron's rod.

The mountain hemlock extends an almost continuous belt along the Sierra and northern ranges to Prince William's Sound, accompanied part of the way by the pines; our two silver firs, to Mount Shasta, thence the fir belt is continued through Oregon, Washington, and British Columbia by four other species, *Abies nobilis*, *grandis*, *amabilis*, and *lasiocarpa*; while the magnificent Sitka spruce, with large, bright purple flowers, adorns the coast region from California to Cook's Inlet and Kodiak. All these, interblending, form one flowery belt — one garden blooming in June, rocking its myriad spires in the hearty weather, bowing and swirling, enjoying clouds and the winds and filling them with balsam; covering thousands of miles of the wildest mountains, clothing the long slopes by the sea, crowning bluffs and headlands and innumerable islands and, fringing the banks of the glaciers, one wild wavering belt of the noblest flowers in the world worth a lifetime of love work to know it.

California Grizzly Bear. From Drawing By F. O. C. Darley.

AMONG THE ANIMALS OF THE YOSEMITE.

THE Sierra bear, brown or gray, the sequoia of the animals, tramps over all the park, though few travelers have the pleasure of seeing him. On he fares through the majestic forests and cañons, facing all sorts of weather, rejoicing in his strength, everywhere at home, harmonizing with the trees and rocks and shaggy chaparral. Happy fellow! his lines have fallen in pleasant places, — lily gardens in silver-fir forests, miles of bushes in endless variety and exuberance of bloom over hill-waves and valleys and along the banks of streams, cañons full of music and waterfalls, parks fair as Eden, — places in which one might expect to meet angels rather than bears.

In this happy land no famine comes nigh him. All the year round his bread is sure, for some of the thousand kinds that he likes are always in season and accessible, ranged on the shelves of the mountains like stores in a pantry. From one to another, from climate to climate, up and down he climbs, feasting on each in turn, — enjoying as great variety as if he traveled to far-off countries north and south. To him almost everything is food except granite. Every tree helps to feed him, every bush and herb, with fruits and flowers, leaves and bark; and all the animals he can catch, — badgers, gophers, ground squirrels, lizards, snakes, etc., and ants, bees, wasps, old and young, together with their eggs and larvæ and nests. Craunched and hashed, down all go to his marvelous stomach, and vanish as if cast into a fire. What digestion! A sheep or a wounded deer or a pig he eats warm, about as quickly as a boy eats a buttered muffin; or should the meat be a month old, it still is welcomed with tremendous relish. After so gross a meal as this, perhaps the next will be strawberries and clover, or raspberries with mushrooms and nuts, or puckery acorns and chokecherries. And as if fearing that anything eatable in all his dominions should escape being eaten, he breaks into cabins to look after sugar, dried apples, bacon, etc. Occasionally he eats the mountaineer's bed; but when he has had a full meal of more tempting dainties he usually leaves it undisturbed, though he has been known to drag it up through a hole in the roof, carry it to the foot of a tree, and lie down on it to enjoy a siesta. Eating everything, never is he himself eaten except by man, and only man is an enemy to be feared. "B'ar meat," said a hunter from whom I was seeking information, "b'ar meat is the best meat in the mountains; their skins make the best beds, and their grease the best butter. Biscuit shortened with b'ar grease goes as far as beans; a man will walk all day on a couple of them biscuit."

In my first interview with a Sierra bear we were frightened and embarrassed, both of us, but the bear's behavior was better than mine. When I discovered him, he was standing in a narrow strip of meadow, and I was concealed behind a tree on the side of it. After studying his appearance as he stood at rest, I rushed toward him to frighten him, that I might study his gait in running. But, contrary to all I had heard about the shyness of bears, he did not run at all; and when I stopped short within a few steps of him, as he held his ground in a fighting attitude, my mistake was monstrously plain. I was then put on my good behavior, and never afterward forgot the right manners of the wilderness.

This happened on my first Sierra excursion in the forest to the north of Yosemite Valley. I was eager to meet the animals, and many of them came to me as if willing to show themselves and make my acquaintance; but the bears kept out of my way.

An old mountaineer, in reply to my questions, told me that bears were very shy, all save grim old grizzlies, and that I might travel the mountains for years without seeing one, unless I gave my mind to them and practiced the stealthy ways of hunters. Nevertheless, it was only a few weeks after I had received this information that I met the one mentioned above, and obtained instruction at first-hand.

I was encamped in the woods about a mile back of the rim of Yosemite, beside a stream that falls into the valley by the way of Indian Cañon. Nearly every day for weeks I went to the top of the North Dome to sketch; for it commands a general view of the valley, and I was anxious to draw every tree and rock and waterfall. Carlo, a St. Bernard dog, was my companion, — a fine, intelligent fellow that belonged to a hunter who was compelled to remain all summer on the hot plains, and who loaned him to me for the season for the sake of having him in the mountains, where he would be so much better off. Carlo knew bears through long experience, and he it was who led me to my first interview, though he seemed as much surprised as the bear at my unhunter-like behavior. One morning in June, just as the sunbeams began to stream through the trees, I set out for a day's sketching on the dome; and before we had gone half a mile from camp Carlo snuffed the air and looked cautiously ahead, lowered his bushy tail, drooped his ears, and began to step softly like a cat, turning every few yards and looking me in the face with a telling expression, saying plainly enough, "There is a bear a little way ahead." I walked carefully in the indicated direction, until I approached a small flowery meadow that I was familiar with, then crawled to the foot of a tree on its margin, bearing in mind what I had been told about the shyness of bears. Looking out cautiously over the instep of the tree, I saw a big, burly cinnamon bear, about thirty yards off, half erect, his paws resting on the trunk of a fir that had fallen into the meadow, his hips almost buried in grass and flowers. He was listening attentively and trying to catch the scent, showing that in some way he was aware of our approach. I watched his gestures, and tried to make the most of my opportunity to learn what I could about him, fearing he would not stay long. He made a fine picture, standing alert in the sunny garden walled in by the most beautiful firs in the world.

After examining him at leisure, noting the sharp muzzle thrust inquiringly forward, the long shaggy hair on his broad chest, the stiff ears nearly buried in hair, and the slow, heavy way in which he moved his head, I foolishly made a rush on him, throwing up my arms and shouting to frighten him, to see him run. He did not mind the demonstration much; only pushed his head farther forward, and looked at me sharply as if asking, "What now? If you want to fight, I'm ready." Then I began to fear that on me would fall the work of running. But I was afraid to run, lest he should be encouraged to pursue me; therefore I held my ground, staring him in the face within a dozen yards or so, putting on as bold a look as I could, and hoping the influence of the human eye would be as great as it is said to be. Under these strained relations the interview seemed to last a long time. Finally, the bear, seeing how still I was, calmly withdrew his huge paws from the log, gave me a piercing look as if warning me not to follow him, turned, and walked slowly up the middle of the meadow into the forest; stopping every few steps and looking back to make sure that I was not trying to take him at a disadvantage in a rear attack. I was glad to part with him, and greatly enjoyed the vanishing view as he waded through the lilies and columbines.

Thenceforth I always tried to give bears respectful notice of my approach, and they usually kept well out of my way. Though they often came around my camp in the night, only once afterward, as far as I know, was I very near one of them in daylight. This time it was a grizzly I met; and as luck would have it, I was even nearer to him than I had been to the big cinnamon. Though not a large specimen, he seemed formidable enough at a distance of less than a dozen yards. His shaggy coat was well grizzled, his head almost white. When I first caught sight of him he was eating acorns under a Kellogg oak, at a distance of perhaps seventy-five yards, and I tried to slip past without disturbing him. But he had either heard my steps on the gravel or caught my scent, for he came straight toward me, stopping every rod or so to look and listen; and as I was afraid to be seen running, I crawled on my hands and knees a little way to one side and hid behind a libocedrus, hoping he would pass me unnoticed. He soon came up opposite me, and stood looking ahead, while I looked at him, peering past the bulging trunk of the tree. At last, turning his head, he caught sight of mine, stared sharply a minute or two, and then, with fine dignity, disappeared in a manzanita-covered earthquake talus.

Considering how heavy and broad-footed bears are, it is wonderful how little harm they do in the wilderness. Even in the well-watered gardens of the middle region, where the flowers grow tallest, and where during warm weather the bears wallow and roll, no evidence of destruction is visible. On the contrary, under nature's direction, the massive beasts act as gardeners. On the forest floor, carpeted with needles and brush, and on the tough sod of glacier meadows, bears make no mark, but around the sandy margin of lakes their magnificent tracks form grand lines of embroidery. Their well-worn trails extend along the main cañons on either side, and though dusty in some places make no scar on the landscape. They bite and break off the branches of some of the pines and oaks to get the nuts, but this pruning is so light that few mountaineers ever notice it; and though they interfere with the orderly lichen-veiled decay of fallen trees, tearing them to pieces to reach the colonies of ants that inhabit them, the scattered ruins are quickly pressed back into harmony by snow and rain and overleaning vegetation.

The number of bears that make the park their home may be guessed by the number that have been killed by the two best hunters, Duncan and old David Brown. Duncan began to be known as a bear-killer about the year 1865. He was then roaming the woods, hunting and prospecting on the south fork of the Merced. A friend told me that he killed his first bear near his cabin at Wawona; that after mustering courage to fire he fled, without waiting to learn the effect of his shot. Going back in a few hours he found poor Bruin dead, and gained courage to try again. Duncan confessed to me, when we made an excursion together in 1875, that he was at first mortally afraid of bears, but after killing a half dozen he began to keep count of his victims, and became ambitious to be known as a great bear-hunter. In nine years he had killed forty-nine, keeping count by notches cut on one of the timbers of his cabin on the shore of Crescent Lake, near the south boundary of the park. He said the more he knew about bears, the more he respected them and the less he feared them. But at the same time he grew more and more cautious, and never fired until he had every advantage, no matter how long he had to wait and how far he had to go before he got the bear just right as to the direction of the wind, the distance, and the way of escape in case of accident; making allowance also for the character of the animal, old or young, cinnamon or grizzly. For old grizzlies, he said, he had no use whatever, and he was mighty careful to avoid their acquaintance. He wanted to kill an even hundred; then he was going to confine himself to safer game. There was not much money in bears, anyhow, and a round hundred was enough for glory.

I have not seen or heard of him lately, and do not know how his bloody count stands. On my excursions, I occasionally passed his cabin. It was full of meat and skins hung in bundles from the rafters, and the ground about it was strewn with bones and hair, — infinitely less tidy than a bear's den. He went as hunter and guide with a geological survey party for a year or two, and was very proud of the scientific knowledge he picked up. His admiring fellow mountaineers, he said, gave him credit for knowing not only the botanical names of all the trees and bushes, but also the "botanical names of the bears."

The most famous hunter of the region was David Brown, an old pioneer, who early in the gold period established his main camp in a little forest glade on the north fork of the Merced, which is still called "Brown's Flat." No finer solitude for a hunter and prospector could be found; the climate is delightful all the year, and the scenery of both earth and sky is a perpetual feast. Though he was not much of a "scenery fellow," his friends say that he knew a pretty place when he saw it as well as any one, and liked mightily to get on the top of a commanding ridge to "look off."

When out of provision, he would take down his old-fashioned long-barreled rifle from its deer-horn rest over the fireplace and set out in search of game. Seldom did he have to go far for venison, because the deer liked the wooded slopes of Pilot Peak ridge, with its open spots where they could rest and look about them, and enjoy the breeze from the sea in warm weather, free from troublesome flies, while they found hiding-places and fine aromatic food in the deer-brush chaparral. A small, wise dog was his only companion, and well the little mountaineer understood the object of every hunt, whether deer or bears, or only grouse hidden in the fir-tops. In deer-hunting Sandy had little to do, trotting behind his master as he walked noiselessly through the fragrant woods, careful not to step heavily on dry twigs, scanning open spots in the chaparral where the deer feed in the early morning and toward sunset, peering over ridges and swells as new outlooks were reached, and along alder and willow fringed flats and streams, until he found a young buck, killed it, tied its legs together, threw it on his shoulder, and so back to camp. But when bears were hunted, Sandy played an important part as leader, and several times saved his master's life; and it was as a bear-hunter that David Brown became famous. His method, as I had it from a friend who had passed many an evening in his cabin listening to his long stories of adventure, was simply to take a few pounds of flour and his rifle, and go slowly and silently over hill and valley in the loneliest part of the wilderness, until little Sandy came upon the fresh track of a bear, then follow it to the death, paying no heed to time. Wherever the bear went he went, however rough the ground, led by Sandy, who looked back from time to time to see how his master was coming on, and regulated his pace accordingly, never growing weary or allowing any other track to divert him. When high ground was reached a halt was made, to scan the openings in every direction, and perchance Bruin would be discovered sitting upright on his haunches, eating manzanita berries; pulling down the fruit-laden branches with his paws and pressing them together, so as to get substantial mouthfuls, however mixed with leaves and twigs. The time of year enabled the hunter to determine approximately where the game would be found: in spring and early summer, in lush grass and clover meadows and in berry tangles along the banks of streams, or on pea-vine and lupine clad slopes; in late summer and autumn, beneath the pines, eating the cones cut off by the squirrels, and in oak groves at the bottom of cañons, munching acorns, manzanita berries, and cherries; and after snow had fallen, in alluvial bottoms, feeding on ants and yellow-jacket wasps. These food places were always cautiously approached, so as to avoid the chance of sudden encounters.

"Whenever," said the hunter, "I saw a bear before he saw me, I had no trouble in killing him. I just took lots of time to learn what he was up to and how long he would be likely to stay, and to study the direction of the wind and the lay of the land. Then I worked round to leeward of him, no matter how far I had to go; crawled and dodged to within a hundred yards, near the foot of a tree that I could climb, but which was too small for a bear to climb. There I looked well to the priming of my rifle, took off my boots so as to climb quickly if necessary, and, with my rifle in rest and Sandy behind me, waited until my bear stood right, when I made a sure, or at least a good shot back of the fore leg. In case he showed fight, I got up the tree I had in mind, before he could reach me. But bears are slow and awkward with their eyes, and being to windward they could not scent me, and often I got in a second shot before they saw the smoke. Usually, however, they tried to get away when they were hurt, and I let them go a good safe while before I ventured into the brush after them. Then Sandy was pretty sure to find them dead; if not, he barked bold as a lion to draw attention, or rushed in and nipped them behind, enabling me to get to a safe distance and watch a chance for a finishing shot."

"Oh yes, bear-hunting is a mighty interesting business, and safe enough if followed just right, though, like every other business, especially the wild kind, it has its accidents, and Sandy and I have had close calls at times. Bears are nobody's fools, and they know enough to let men alone as a general thing, unless they are wounded, or cornered, or have cubs. In my opinion, a hungry old mother would catch and eat a man, if she could; which is only fair play, anyhow, for we eat them. But nobody, as far as I know, has been eaten up in these rich mountains. Why they never tackle a fellow when he is lying asleep I never could understand. They could gobble us mighty handy, but I suppose it's nature to respect a sleeping man."

Sheep-owners and their shepherds have killed a great many bears, mostly by poison and traps of various sorts. Bears are fond of mutton, and levy heavy toll on every flock driven into the mountains. They usually come to the corral at night, climb in, kill a sheep with a stroke of the paw, carry it off a little distance, eat about half of it, and return the next night for the other half; and so on all summer, or until they are themselves killed. It is not, however, by direct killing, but by suffocation through crowding against the corral wall in fright, that the greatest losses are incurred. From ten to fifteen sheep are found dead, smothered in the corral, after every attack; or the walls are broken, and the flock is scattered far and wide. A flock may escape the attention of these marauders for a week or two in the spring; but after their first taste of the fine mountain-fed meat the visits are persistently kept up, in spite of all precautions. Once I spent a night with two Portuguese shepherds, who were greatly troubled with bears, from two to four or five visiting them almost every night. Their camp was near the middle of the park, and the wicked bears, they said, were getting worse and worse. Not waiting now until dark, they came out of the brush in broad daylight, and boldly carried off as many sheep as they liked. One evening, before sundown, a bear, followed by two cubs, came for an early supper, as the flock was being slowly driven toward camp. Joe, the elder of the shepherds, warned by many exciting experiences, promptly climbed a tall tamarack pine, and left the freebooters to help themselves; while Antone, calling him a coward, and declaring that he was not going to let bears eat up his sheep before his face, set the dogs on them, and rushed toward them with a great noise and a stick. The frightened cubs ran up a tree, and the mother ran to meet the shepherd and dogs. Antone stood astonished for a moment, eying the oncoming bear; then fled faster than Joe had, closely pursued. He scrambled to the roof of their little cabin, the only refuge quickly available; and fortunately, the bear, anxious about her young, did not climb after him, — only held him in mortal terror a few minutes, glaring and threatening, then hastened back to her cubs, called them down, went to the frightened, huddled flock, killed a sheep, and feasted in peace. Antone piteously entreated cautious Joe to show him a good safe tree, up which he climbed like a sailor climbing a mast, and held on as long as he could with legs crossed, the slim pine recommended by Joe being nearly branchless. "So you too are a bear coward, as well as Joe," I said, after hearing the story. "Oh, I tell you," he replied, with grand solemnity, "bear face close by look awful; she just as soon eat me as not. She do so as eef all my sheeps b'long every one to her own self. I run to bear no more. I take tree every time."

After this the shepherds corralled the flock about an hour before sundown, chopped large quantities of dry wood and made a circle of fires around the corral every night, and one with a gun kept watch on a stage built in a pine by the side of the cabin, while the other slept. But after the first night or two this fire fence did no good, for the robbers seemed to regard the light as an advantage, after becoming used to it.

On the night I spent at their camp the show made by the wall of fire when it was blazing in its prime was magnificent: the illumined trees round about relieved against solid darkness, and the two thousand sheep lying down in one gray mass, sprinkled with gloriously brilliant gems, the effect of the firelight in their eyes. It was nearly midnight when a pair of the freebooters arrived. They walked boldly through a gap in the fire circle, killed two sheep, carried them out, and vanished in the dark woods, leaving ten dead in a pile, trampled down and smothered against the corral fence; while the scared watcher in the tree did not fire a single shot, saying he was afraid he would hit some of the sheep, as the bears got among them before he could get a good sight.

In the morning I asked the shepherds why they did not move the flock to a new pasture. "Oh, no use!" cried Antone. "Look my dead sheeps. We move three four time before, all the same bear come by the track. No use. To-morrow we go home below. Look my dead sheeps. Soon all dead."

Thus were they driven out of the mountains more than a month before the usual time. After Uncle Sam's soldiers, bears are the most effective forest police, but some of the shepherds are very successful in killing them. Altogether, by hunters, mountaineers, Indians, and sheepmen, probably five or six hundred have been killed within the bounds of the park, during the last thirty years. But they are not in danger of extinction. Now that the park is guarded by soldiers, not only has the vegetation in great part come back to the desolate ground, but all the wild animals are increasing in numbers. No guns are allowed in the park except under certain restrictions, and after a permit has been obtained from the officer in charge. This has stopped the barbarous slaughter of bears, and especially of deer, by shepherds, hunters, and hunting tourists, who, it would seem, can find no pleasure without blood.

The Sierra deer — the blacktail — spend the winters in the brushy and exceedingly rough region just below the main timber-belt, and are less accessible to hunters there than when they are passing through the comparatively open forests to and from their summer pastures near the summits of the range. They go up the mountains early in the spring as the snow melts, not waiting for it all to disappear; reaching the High Sierra about the first of June, and the coolest recesses at the base of the peaks a month or so later. I have tracked them for miles over compacted snow from three to ten feet deep.

Deer are capital mountaineers, making their way into the heart of the roughest mountains; seeking not only pasturage, but a cool climate, and safe hidden places in which to bring forth their young. They are not supreme as rock-climbing animals; they take second rank, yielding the first to the mountain sheep, which dwell above them on the highest crags and peaks. Still, the two meet frequently; for the deer climbs all the peaks save the lofty summits above the glaciers, crossing piles of angular boulders, roaring swollen streams, and sheer-walled cañons by fords and passes that would try the nerves of the hardiest mountaineers, — climbing with graceful ease and reserve of strength that cannot fail to arouse admiration. Everywhere some species of deer seems to be at home, on rough or smooth ground, lowlands or highlands, in swamps and barrens and the densest woods, in varying climates, hot or cold, over all the continent; maintaining glorious health, never making an awkward step. Standing, lying down, walking, feeding, running even for life, it is always invincibly graceful, and adds beauty and animation to every landscape, —

a charming animal, and a great credit to nature.

I never see one of the common black-tail deer, the only species in the park, without fresh admiration; and since I never carry a gun I see them well: lying beneath a juniper or dwarf pine, among the brown needles on the brink of some cliff or the end of a ridge commanding a wide outlook; feeding in sunny openings among chaparral, daintily selecting aromatic leaves and twigs; leading their fawns out of my way, or making them lie down and hide; bounding past through the forest, or curiously advancing and retreating again and again.

One morning when I was eating breakfast in a little garden spot on the Kaweah, hedged around with chaparral, I noticed a deer's head thrust through the bushes, the big beautiful eyes gazing at me. I kept still, and the deer ventured forward a step, then snorted and withdrew. In a few minutes she returned, and came into the open garden, stepping with infinite grace, followed by two others. After showing themselves for a moment, they bounded over the hedge with sharp, timid snorts and vanished. But curiosity brought them back with still another, and all four came into my garden, and, satisfied that I meant them no ill, began to feed, actually eating breakfast with me, like tame, gentle sheep around a shepherd, — rare company, and the most graceful in movements and attitudes. I eagerly watched them while they fed on ceanothus and wild cherry, daintily culling single leaves here and there from the side of the hedge, turning now and then to snip a few leaves of mint from the midst of the garden flowers. Grass they did not eat at all. No wonder the contents of the deer's stomach are eaten by the Indians.

While exploring the upper cañon of the north fork of the San Joaquin, one evening, the sky threatening rain, I searched for a dry bed, and made choice of a big juniper that had been pushed down by a snow avalanche, but was resting stubbornly on its knees high enough to let me lie under its broad trunk. Just below my shelter there was another juniper on the very brink of a precipice, and, examining it, I found a deer-bed beneath it, completely protected and concealed by drooping branches, — a fine refuge and lookout as well as resting-place. About an hour before dark I heard the clear, sharp snorting of a deer, and looking down on the brushy, rocky cañon bottom discovered an anxious doe that no doubt had her fawns concealed near by. She bounded over the chaparral and up the farther slope of the wall, often stopping to look back and listen, — a fine picture of vivid, eager alertness. I sat perfectly still, and as my shirt was colored like the juniper bark I was not easily seen. After a little she came cautiously toward me, sniffing the air and gazing, and her movements, as she descended the cañon side over boulder piles and brush and fallen timber, were admirably strong and beautiful; she never strained or made apparent efforts, although jumping high here and there. As she drew nigh she sniffed anxiously, trying the air in different directions until she caught my scent; then bounded off, and vanished behind a small grove of firs. Soon she came back with the same caution and insatiable curiosity, — coming and going five or six times. While I sat admiring her, a Douglas squirrel, evidently excited by her noisy alarms, climbed a boulder beneath me, and witnessed her performances as attentively as I did, while a frisky chipmunk, too restless or hungry for such shows, busied himself about his supper in a thicket of shadbushes, the fruit of which was then ripe, glancing about on the slender twigs lightly as a sparrow.

Toward the end of the Indian summer, when the young are strong, the deer begin to gather in little bands of from six to fifteen or twenty, and on the approach of the first snowstorm they set out on

"Crossing the Chowchilla Ridge."

A Coyote Howling

their march down the mountains to their winter quarters; lingering usually on warm hillsides and spurs eight or ten miles below the summits, as if loath to leave. About the end of November, a heavy, far-reaching storm drives them down in haste along the dividing ridges between the rivers, led by old experienced bucks whose knowledge of the topography is wonderful.

It is when the deer are coming down that the Indians set out on their grand fall hunt. Too lazy to go into the recesses of the mountains away from trails, they wait for the deer to come out, and then waylay them. This plan also has the advantage of finding them in bands. Great preparations are made. Old guns are mended, bullets moulded, and the hunters wash themselves and fast to some extent, to insure good luck, as they say. Men and women, old and young, set forth together. Central camps are made on the well-known highways of the deer, which are soon red with blood. Each hunter comes in laden, old crones as well as maidens smiling on the luckiest. All grow fat and merry. Boys, each armed with an antlered head, play at buck-fighting, and plague the industrious women, who are busily preparing the meat for transportation, by stealing up behind them and throwing fresh hides over them. But the Indians are passing away here as everywhere, and their red camps on the mountains are fewer every year.

There are panthers, foxes, badgers, porcupines, and coyotes in the park, but not in large numbers. I have seen coyotes well back in the range at the head of the Tuolumne Meadows as early as June 1st, before the snow was gone, feeding on marmots; but they are far more numerous on the inhabited lowlands around ranches, where they enjoy life on chickens, turkeys, quail eggs, ground squirrels, hares, etc., and all kinds of fruit. Few wild sheep, I fear, are left hereabouts; for, though safe on the high peaks, they are driven down the eastern slope of the mountains when the deer are driven down the western, to ridges and outlying spurs where the snow does not fall to a great depth, and there they are within reach of the cattlemen's rifles.

The two squirrels of the park, the Douglas and the California gray, keep all the woods lively. The former is far more abundant and more widely distributed, being found all the way up from the foothills to the dwarf pines on the summit peaks. He is the most influential of the Sierra animals, though small, and the brightest of all the squirrels I know, — a squirrel of squirrels, quick mountain vigor and valor condensed, purely wild, and as free from disease as a sunbeam. One cannot think of such an animal ever being weary or sick. He claims all the woods, and is inclined to drive away even men as intruders. How he scolds, and what faces he makes! If not so comically small, he would be a dreadful fellow. The gray, *Sciurus fossor*, is the handsomest, I think, of all the large American squirrels. He is something like the Eastern gray, but is brighter and clearer in color, and more lithe and slender. He dwells in the oak and pine woods up to a height of about five thousand feet above the sea, is rather common in Yosemite Valley, Hetch-Hetchy, Kings River Cañon, and indeed in all the main cañons and Yosemites, but does not like the high fir-covered ridges. Compared with the Douglas, the gray is more than twice as large; nevertheless, he manages to make his way through the trees with less stir than his small, peppery neighbor, and is much less influential in every way. In the spring, before pine-nuts and hazel-nuts are ripe, he examines last year's cones for the few seeds that may be left in them between the half-open scales, and gleans fallen nuts and seeds on the ground among the leaves, after making sure that no enemy is nigh. His fine tail floats, now behind, now above him, level or gracefully curled, light and radiant as dry thistledown. His body seems hardly more substantial than his tail. The Douglas is a firm, emphatic bolt of life, fiery, pungent, full of brag and show and fight, and his movements have none of the elegant deliberation of the gray. They are so quick and keen they almost sting the onlooker, and the acrobatic harlequin gyrating show he makes of himself turns one giddy to see. The gray is shy and oftentimes stealthy, as if half expecting to find an enemy in every tree and bush and behind every log; he seems to wish to be let alone, and manifests no desire to be seen, or admired, or feared. He is hunted by the Indians, and this of itself is cause enough for caution. The Douglas is less attractive as game, and is probably increasing in numbers in spite of every enemy. He goes his ways bold as a lion, up and down and across, round and round, the happiest, merriest, of all the hairy tribe, and at the same time tremendously earnest and solemn, sunshine incarnate, making every tree tingle with his electric toes. If you prick him, you cannot think he will bleed. He seems above the chance and change that beset common mortals, though in busily gathering burs and nuts he shows that he has to work for a living, like the rest of us. I never found a dead Douglas. He gets into the world and out of it without being noticed; only in prime is he seen, like some little plants that are visible only when in bloom.

The Townsend tamias, a plump, slow, sober, well-dressed chipmunk, nearly as large as the Douglas squirrel, may occasionally be seen about the roots of the firs or fallen trunks, solemnly staring as if he never had anything to do. The little striped species, *T. quadrivittatus*, is more interesting and a hundred times more numerous than the Townsend. A brighter, cheerier chipmunk does not exist. He is smarter, more arboreal and squirrel-like, than the familiar Eastern species, and is distributed as widely on the Sierra as the Douglas. Every forest however dense or open, every hilltop and cañon however brushy or bare, is cheered and enlivened by this happy little animal. You are likely to notice him first on the lower edge of the coniferous belt, where the sabine and yellow pines meet; and thence upward, go where you may, you will find him every day, even in winter, unless the weather is stormy. He is an exceedingly interesting little fellow, full of odd, quaint ways, confiding, thinking no evil; and without being a squirrel — a true shadow-tail — he lives the life of a squirrel, and has almost all squirrelish accomplishments without aggressive quarrelsomeness.

I never weary of watching him as he frisks about in the bushes, gathering seeds and berries; poising on slender twigs of wild cherry, shad, chinquapin, buckthorn bramble; skimming along prostrate trunks or over the grassy, needle-strewn forest floor; darting from boulder to boulder on glacial pavements and the tops of the great domes. When the seeds of the conifers are ripe, he climbs the trees and cuts off the cones for a winter store, working diligently, though not with the tremendous lightning energy of the Douglas, who frequently drives him out of the best trees. Then he lies in wait, and picks up a share of the burs cut off by his domineering cousin, and stores them beneath logs and in hollows. Few of the Sierra animals are so well liked as this little airy, fluffy half squirrel, half spermophile. So gentle, confiding, and busily cheery and happy, he takes one's heart and keeps his place among the best loved of the mountain darlings. A diligent collector of seeds, nuts, and berries, of course he is well fed, though never in the least dumpy with fat. On the contrary, he looks like a mere fluff of fur, weighing but little more than a field mouse, and of his frisky, birdlike liveliness without haste there is no end. Douglas can bark with his mouth closed, but little quad always opens his when he talks or sings. He has a considerable variety of notes which correspond with his movements, some of them sweet and liquid, like water dripping into a pool with tinkling sound. His eyes are black and animated, shining like dew. He seems dearly to like teasing a dog, venturing within a few feet of it, then frisking away with a lively chipping and low squirrelish churring; beating time to his music, such as it is, with his tail, which at each chip and churr describes a half circle. Not even Douglas is surer-footed or takes greater risks. I have seen him running about on sheer Yosemite cliffs, holding on with as little effort as a fly and as little thought of danger in places where, if he had made the least slip, he would have fallen thousands of feet. How fine it would be could mountaineers move about on precipices with the same sure grip!

Before the pine-nuts are ripe, grass seeds and those of the many species of ceanothus, with strawberries, raspberries, and the soft red thimbleberries of *Rubus nutkanus*, form the bulk of his food, and a neater eater is not to be found in the mountains. Bees powdered with pollen, poking their blunt noses into the bells of flowers, are comparatively clumsy and boorish. Frisking along some fallen pine or fir, when the grass seeds are ripe, he looks about him, considering which of the tufts he sees is likely to have the best, runs out to it, selects what he thinks is sure to be a good head, cuts it off, carries it to the top of the log, sits upright and nibbles out the grain without getting awns in his mouth, turning the head round, holding it and fingering it as if playing on a flute; then skips for another and another, bringing them to the same dining-log.

The woodchuck — *Arctomys monax* — dwells on high bleak ridges and boulder piles; and a very different sort of mountaineer is he. — bulky, fat, aldermanic.

and fairly bloated at times by hearty indulgence in the lush pastures of his airy home. And yet he is by no means a dull animal. In the midst of what we regard as storm-beaten desolation, high in the frosty air, beside the glaciers, he pipes and whistles right cheerily, and lives to a good old age. If you are as early a riser as he is, you may oftentimes see him come blinking out of his burrow to meet the first beams of the morning and take a sunbath on some favorite flat-topped boulder. Afterward, well warmed, he goes to breakfast in one of his garden hollows, eats heartily like a cow in clover until comfortably swollen, then goes a-visiting, and plays and loves and fights.

In the spring of 1875, when I was exploring the peaks and glaciers about the head of the middle fork of the San Joaquin, I had crossed the range from the head of Owen River, and one morning, passing around a frozen lake where the snow was perhaps ten feet deep, I was surprised to find the fresh track of a woodchuck plainly marked, the sun having softened the surface. What could the animal be thinking of, coming out so early while all the ground was snow-buried? The steady trend of his track showed he had a definite aim, and fortunately it was toward a mountain thirteen thousand feet high that I meant to climb. So I followed to see if I could find out what he was up to. From the base of the mountain the track pointed straight up, and I knew by the melting snow that I was not far behind him. I lost the track on a crumbling ridge, partly projecting through the snow, but soon discovered it again. Well toward the summit of the mountain, in an open spot on the south side, nearly inclosed by disintegrating pinnacles among which the sun heat reverberated, making an isolated patch of warm climate, I found a nice garden, full of rock cress, phlox, silene, draba, etc., and a few grasses; and in this garden I overtook the wanderer, enjoying a fine fresh meal, perhaps the first of the season. How did he know the way to this one garden spot, so high and far off, and what told him that it was in bloom while yet the snow was ten feet deep over his den? For this it would seem he would need more botanical, topographical, and climatological knowledge than most mountaineers are possessed of.

The shy, curious mountain beaver — *Haplodon* — lives on the heights, not far from the woodchuck. He digs canals and controls the flow of small streams under the sod, cuts large quantities of grass, lupines, and other plants, lays them out in neat piles with the stems all one way to dry, like hay, and stores them in underground chambers. These hayfields on the mountain tops, showing busy, thoughtful life where one deemed himself alone, are startling. And it is startling, too, when one is camped on the edge of a sloping meadow near the homes of these industrious mountaineers, to be awakened in the still night by the sound of water rushing and gurgling under one's head in a newly formed canal. Pouched gophers also have a way of awakening nervous campers that is quite as exciting as the haplodon's plan; that is, by a series of firm upward pushes when they are driving tunnels and shoving up the dirt. One naturally cries out, "Who 's there?" and then discovering the cause, "All right. Go on. Goodnight," and goes to sleep again.

The wood rat — *Neotoma* — is one of the most interesting of the Sierra animals. He is scarcely at all like the common rat, is nearly twice as large, has a delicate soft fur of a bluish slate color, white on the belly, large ears thin and translucent, eyes full and liquid and mild in expression, nose blunt and squirrelish, slender claws sharp as needles, and as his limbs are strong he can climb about as well as a squirrel; while no rat or squirrel has so innocent a look, is so easily approached, or in general expresses so much confidence in one's good intentions. He seems too fine for the thorny thickets he inhabits, and his big, rough hut is as unlike himself as possible. No other animal in these mountains makes nests so large and striking in appearance as his. They are built of all kinds of sticks (broken branches, and old rotten moss-grown chunks, and green twigs, smooth or thorny, cut from the nearest bushes), mixed with miscellaneous rubbish and curious odds and ends, — bits of cloddy earth, stones, bones, bits of deer-horn, etc.: the whole simply piled in conical masses on the ground in chaparral thickets. Some of these cabins are five or six feet high, and occasionally a dozen or more are grouped together; less, perhaps, for society's sake than for advantages of food and shelter.

Coming through deep, stiff chaparral in the heart of the wilderness, heated and weary in forcing a way, the solitary explorer, happening into one of these curious neotoma villages, is startled at the strange sight, and may imagine he is in an Indian village, and feel anxious as to the reception he will get in a place so wild. At first, perhaps, not a single inhabitant will be seen, or at most only two or three seated on the tops of their huts as at the doors, observing the stranger with the mildest of mild eyes. The nest in the centre of the cabin is made of grass and films of bark chewed to tow, and lined with feathers and the down of various seeds. The thick, rough walls seem to be built for defense against enemies — fox, coyote, etc. — as well as for shelter, and the delicate creatures, in their big, rude homes, suggest tender flowers, like those of *Salvia carduacea*, defended by thorny involucres.

Sometimes the home is built in the forks of an oak, twenty or thirty feet from the ground, and even in garrets. Among housekeepers who have these bushmen as neighbors or guests they are regarded as thieves, because they carry away and pile together everything transportable (knives, forks, tin cups, spoons, spectacles, combs, nails, kindling-wood, etc., as well as eatables of all sorts), to strengthen their fortifications or to shine among rivals. Once, far back in the High Sierra, they stole my snow-goggles, the lid of my teapot, and my aneroid barometer; and one stormy night, when encamped under a prostrate cedar, I was awakened by a gritting sound on the granite, and by the light of my fire I discovered a handsome neotoma beside me, dragging away my ice-hatchet, pulling with might and main by a buckskin string on the handle. I threw bits of bark at him and made a noise to frighten him, but he stood scolding and chattering back at me, his fine eyes shining with an air of injured innocence.

A great variety of lizards enliven the warm portions of the park. Some of them are more than a foot in length, others but little larger than grasshoppers. A few are snaky and repulsive at first sight, but most of the species are handsome and attractive, and bear acquaintance well; we like them better the farther we see into their charming lives. Small fellow mortals, gentle and guileless, they are easily tamed, and have beautiful eyes, expressing the clearest innocence, so that, in spite of prejudices brought from cool, lizardless countries, one must soon learn to like them. Even the horned toad of the plains and foothills, called horrid, is mild and gentle, with charming eyes, and so are the snake-like species found in the underbrush of the lower forests. These glide in curves with all the ease and grace of snakes, while their small, undeveloped limbs drag for the most part as useless appendages. One specimen that I measured was fourteen inches long, and as far as I saw it made no use whatever of its diminutive limbs.

Most of them glint and dart on the sunny rocks and across open spaces from bush to bush, swift as dragonflies and humming-birds, and about as brilliantly colored. They never make a long-sustained run, whatever their object, but dart direct as arrows for a distance of ten or twenty feet, then suddenly stop, and as suddenly start again. These stops are necessary as rests, for they are short-winded, and when pursued steadily are soon run out of breath, pant pitifully, and may easily be caught where no retreat in bush or rock is quickly available.

If you stay with them a week or two and behave well, these gentle saurians, descendants of an ancient race of giants, will soon know and trust you, come to your feet, play, and watch your every motion with cunning curiosity. You will surely learn to like them, not only the bright ones, gorgeous as the rainbow, but the little ones, gray as lichened granite, and scarcely bigger than grasshoppers; and they will teach you that scales may cover as fine a nature as hair or feathers or anything tailored.

There are many snakes in the cañons and lower forests, but they are mostly handsome and harmless. Of all the tourists and travelers who have visited Yosemite and the adjacent mountains, not one has been bitten by a snake of any sort, while thousands have been charmed by them. Some of them vie with the lizards in beauty of color and dress patterns. Only the rattlesnake is venomous, and he carefully keeps his venom to himself as far as man is concerned, unless his life is threatened.

Before I learned to respect rattlesnakes I killed two, the first on the San Joaquin plain. He was coiled comfortably around a tuft of bunch-grass, and I discovered him when he was between my feet as I was stepping over him. He held his head down and did not attempt to strike, although in danger of being trampled. At that time, thirty years ago, I imagined that rattlesnakes should be killed wherever found. I had no weapon of any sort, and on the smooth plain there was not a stick or a stone within miles; so I crushed him by jumping on him, as the deer are said to do. Looking me in the face he saw I meant mischief, and quickly cast himself into a coil, ready to strike in defense. I knew he could not strike when traveling, therefore I threw handfuls of dirt and grass sods at him, to tease him out of coil. He held his ground a few minutes, threatening and striking, and then started off to get rid of me. I ran forward and jumped on him; but he drew back his head so quickly my heel missed, and he also missed his stroke at me. Persecuted, tormented, again and again he tried to get away, bravely striking out to protect himself; but at last my heel came squarely down, sorely wounding him, and a few more brutal stampings crushed him. I felt degraded by the

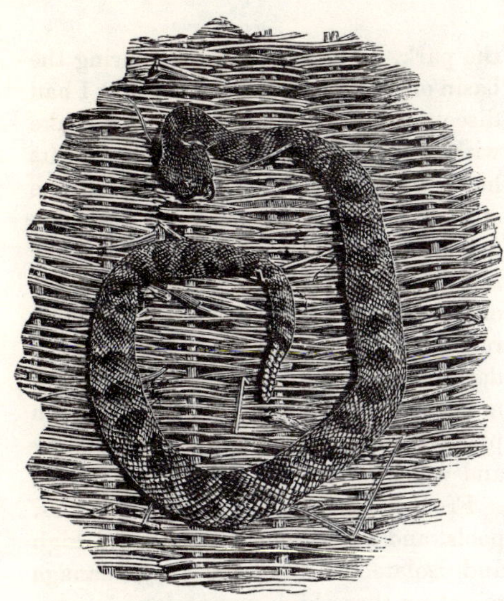

A NATIVE OF THE VALLEY.

killing business, farther from heaven, and I made up my mind to try to be at least as fair and charitable as the snakes themselves, and to kill no more save in self-defense.

The second killing might also, I think, have been avoided, and I have always felt somewhat sore and guilty about it. I had built a little cabin in Yosemite, and for convenience in getting water, and for the sake of music and society, I led a small stream from Yosemite Creek into it. Running along the side of the wall it was not in the way, and it had just fall enough to ripple and sing in low, sweet tones, making delightful company, especially at night when I was lying awake. Then a few frogs came in and made merry with the stream, — and one snake, I suppose to catch the frogs.

Returning from my long walks, I usually brought home a large handful of plants, partly for study, partly for ornament, and set them in a corner of the cabin, with their stems in the stream to keep them fresh. One day, when I picked up a handful that had begun to fade, I uncovered a large coiled rattler that had been hiding behind the flowers. Thus suddenly brought to light face to face with the rightful owner of the place, the poor reptile was desperately embarrassed, evidently realizing that he had no right in the cabin. It was not only fear that he showed, but a good deal of downright bashfulness and embarrassment, like that of a more than half honest person caught under suspicious circumstances behind a door. Instead of striking or threatening to strike, though coiled and ready, he slowly drew his head down as far as he could, with awkward, confused kinks in his neck and a shamefaced expression, as if wishing the ground would open and hide him. I have looked into the eyes of so many wild animals that I feel sure I did not mistake the feelings of this unfortunate snake. I did not want to kill him, but I had many visitors, some of them children, and I oftentimes came in late at night; so I judged he must die.

Since then I have seen perhaps a hundred or more in these mountains, but I have never intentionally disturbed them, nor have they disturbed me to any great extent, even by accident, though in danger of being stepped on. Once, while I was on my knees kindling a fire, one glided under the arch made by my arm. He was only going away from the ground I had selected for a camp, and there was not the slightest danger, because I kept still and allowed him to go in peace. The only time I felt myself in serious danger was when I was coming out of the Tuolumne Cañon by a steep side cañon toward the head of Yosemite Creek. On an earthquake talus, a boulder in my way presented a front so high that I could just reach the upper edge of it while standing on the next below it. Drawing myself up, as soon as my head was above the flat top of it I caught sight of a coiled rattler. My hands had alarmed him, and he was ready for me; but even with this provocation, and when my head came in sight within a foot of him, he did not strike. The last time I sauntered through the big cañon I saw about two a day. One was not coiled, but neatly folded in a narrow space between two cobblestones on the side of the river, his head below the level of them, ready to shoot up like a Jack-in-the-box for frogs or birds. My foot spanned the space above within an inch or two of his head, but he only held it lower. In making my way through a particularly tedious tangle of buckthorn, I parted the branches on the side of an open spot and threw my bundle of bread into it; and when, with my arms free, I was pushing through after it, I saw a small rattlesnake dragging his tail from beneath my bundle. When he caught sight of me he eyed me angrily, and with an air of righteous indignation seemed to be asking why I had thrown that stuff on him. He was so small that I was inclined to slight him, but he struck out so angrily that I drew back, and approached the opening from the other side. But he had been listening, and when I looked through the brush I found him confronting me, still with a come-in-if-you-dare expression. In vain I tried to explain that I only wanted my bread; he stoutly held the ground in front of it; so I went back a dozen rods and kept still for half an hour, and when I returned he had gone.

One evening, near sundown, in a very rough, boulder-choked portion of the cañon, I searched long for a level spot for a bed, and at last was glad to find a patch of flood-sand on the river-bank, and a lot of driftwood close by for a camp-fire. But when I threw down my bundle, I found two snakes in possession of the ground. I might have passed the night even in this snake den without danger, for I never knew a single instance of their coming into camp in the night; but fearing that, in so small a space, some late comers, not aware of my presence, might get stepped on, when I was replenishing the fire, to avoid possible crowding I encamped on one of the earthquake boulders.

There are two species of *Crotalus* in the park, and when I was exploring the basin of Yosemite Creek I thought I had discovered a new one. I saw a snake with curious divided appendages on its head. Going nearer, I found that the strange headgear was only the feet of a frog. Cutting a switch I struck the snake lightly until he disgorged the poor frog, or rather allowed it to back out. On its return to the light from one of the very darkest of death valleys, it blinked a moment with a sort of dazed look, then plunged into a stream, apparently happy and well.

Frogs abound in all the bogs, marshes, pools, and lakes, however cold and high and isolated. How did they manage to get up these high mountains? Surely not by jumping. Long and dry excursions through weary miles of boulders and brush would be trying to frogs. Most likely their stringy spawn is carried on the feet of ducks, cranes, and other waterbirds. Anyhow, they are most thoroughly distributed, and flourish famously. What a cheery, hearty set they are, and how bravely their krink and tronk concerts enliven the rocky wilderness!

None of the high-lying mountain lakes or branches of the rivers above sheer falls had fish of any sort until stocked by the agency of man. In the High Sierra, the only river in which trout exist naturally is the middle fork of Kings River. There are no sheer falls on this stream; some of the rapids, however, are so swift and rough, even at the lowest stage of water, that it is surprising any fish can climb them. I found trout in abundance in this fork up to seventy-five hundred feet. They also run quite high on the Kern. On the Merced they get no higher than Yosemite Valley, four thousand feet, all the forks of the river being barred there by sheer falls, and on the main Tuolumne they are stopped by a fall below Hetch-Hetchy, still lower than Yosemite. Though these upper waters are inaccessible to the fish, one would suppose their eggs might have been planted there by some means. Nature has so many ways of doing such things. In this case she waited for the agency of man, and now many of these hitherto fishless lakes and streams are full of fine trout, stocked by individual enterprise, Walton clubs, etc., in great part under the auspices of the United States Fish Commission. A few trout carried into Hetch-Hetchy in a common water-bucket have multiplied wonderfully fast. Lake Tenaya, at an elevation of over eight thousand feet, was stocked eight years ago by Mr. Murphy, who carried a few trout from Yosemite. Many of the small streams of the eastern slope have also been stocked with trout transported over the passes in tin cans on the backs of mules. Soon, it would seem, all the streams of the range will be enriched by these lively fish, and will become the means of drawing thousands of visitors into the mountains. Catching trout with a bit of bent wire is a rather trivial business, but fortunately people fish better than they know. In most cases it is the man who is caught. Trout-fishing regarded as bait for catching men, for the saving of both body and soul, is important, and deserves all the expense and care bestowed on it.

A Critical Moment.

Sentinel Rock from the North.

AMONG THE BIRDS OF THE YOSEMITE.

TRAVELERS in the Sierra forests usually complain of the want of life. "The trees," they say, "are fine, but the empty stillness is deadly; there are no animals to be seen, no birds. We have not heard a song in all the woods." And no wonder! They go in large parties with mules and horses; they make a great noise; they are dressed in outlandish, unnatural colors: every animal shuns them. Even the frightened pines would run away if they could. But Nature lovers, devout, silent, open-eyed, looking and listening with love, find no lack of inhabitants in these mountain mansions, and they come to them gladly. Not to mention the large animals or the small insect people, every waterfall has its ouzel and every tree its squirrel or tamias or bird: tiny nuthatch threading the furrows of the bark, cheerily whispering to itself as it deftly pries off loose scales and examines the curled edges of lichens; or Clarke crow or jay examining the cones; or some singer — oriole, tanager, warbler — resting, feeding, attending to domestic affairs. Hawks and eagles sail overhead, grouse walk in happy flocks below, and song sparrows sing in every bed of chaparral. There is no crowding, to be sure. Unlike the low Eastern trees, those of the Sierra in the main forest belt average nearly two hundred feet in height, and of course many birds are required to make much show in them and many voices to fill them. Nevertheless, the whole range from foothills to snowy summits is shaken into song every summer; and though low and thin in winter, the music never ceases.

The sage cock — *Centrocercus urophasianus* — is the largest of the Sierra game-birds and the king of American grouse. It is an admirably strong, hardy, handsome, independent bird, able with comfort to bid defiance to heat, cold, drought, hunger, and all sorts of storms, living on whatever seeds or insects chance to come in its way, or simply on the leaves of sage-brush, everywhere abundant on its desert range. In winter, when the temperature is oftentimes below zero, and heavy snowstorms are blowing, he sits beneath a sage bush and allows himself to be covered, poking his head now and then through the snow to feed on the leaves of his shelter. Not even the Arctic ptarmigan is hardier in braving frost and snow and wintry darkness. When in full plumage he is a beautiful bird, with a long, firm, sharp-pointed tail, which in walking is slightly raised and swings sidewise back and forth with each step. The male is handsomely marked with black and white on the neck, back, and wings, weighs five or six pounds, and measures about thirty inches in length. The female is clad mostly in plain brown, and is not so large. They occasionally wander from the sage plains into the open nut-pine and juniper woods, but never enter the main coniferous forest. It is only in the broad, dry, half-desert sage plains that they are quite at home, where the weather is blazing hot in summer, cold in winter. If any one passes through a flock, all squat on the gray ground and hold their heads low, hoping to escape observation; but when approached within a rod or so, they rise with a magnificent burst of wing-beats, looking about as big as turkeys and making a noise like a whirlwind.

On the 28th of June, at the head of Owen's Valley, I caught one of the young that was then just able to fly. It was seven inches long, of a uniform gray color, blunt-billed, and when captured cried lustily in a shrill piping voice, clear in tone as a boy's small willow whistle. I have seen flocks of from ten to thirty or forty on the east margin of the park, where the Mono Desert meets the gray foothills of the Sierra; but since cattle have been pastured there they are becoming rarer every year.

Another magnificent bird, the blue or dusky grouse, next in size to the sage cock, is found all through the main forest belt, though not in great numbers. They like best the heaviest silver-fir woods near garden and meadow openings, where there is but little underbrush to cover the approach of enemies. When a flock of these brave birds, sauntering and feeding on the sunny flowery levels of some hidden meadow or Yosemite valley far back in the heart of the mountains, see a man for the first time in their lives, they rise with hurried notes of surprise and excitement and alight on the lowest branches of the trees, wondering what the wanderer may be, and showing great eagerness to get a good view of the strange vertical animal. Knowing nothing of guns, they allow you to approach within a half dozen paces, then quietly hop a few branches higher or fly to the next tree without a thought of concealment, so that you may observe them as long as you like, near enough to see the fine shading of their plumage, the feathers on their toes, and the innocent wonderment in their beautiful wild eyes. But in the neighborhood of roads and trails they soon become shy, and when disturbed fly into the highest, leafiest trees, and suddenly become invisible, so well do they know how to hide and keep still and make use of their protective coloring. Nor can they be easily dislodged ere they are ready to go. In vain the hunter goes round and round some tall pine or fir into which he has perhaps seen a dozen enter, gazing up through the branches, straining his eyes while his gun is held ready; not a feather can he see unless his eyes have been sharpened by long experience and knowledge of the blue grouse's habits. Then, perhaps, when he is thinking that the tree must be hollow and that the birds have all gone inside, they burst forth with a startling whir of wing-beats, and after gaining full speed go skating swiftly away through the forest arches in a long, silent, wavering slide, with wings held steady.

During the summer they are most of the time on the ground, feeding on insects, seeds, berries, etc., around the margins of open spots and rocky moraines, playing and sauntering, taking sun baths and sand baths, and drinking at little pools and rills during the heat of the day. In winter they live mostly in the trees, depending on buds for food, sheltering beneath dense overlapping branches at night and during storms on the leeside of the trunk, sunning themselves on the southside limbs in fine weather, and sometimes diving into the mealy snow to flutter and wallow, apparently for exercise and fun.

I have seen young broods running beneath the firs in June at a height of eight thousand feet above the sea. On the approach of danger, the mother with a peculiar cry warns the helpless midgets to scatter and hide beneath leaves and twigs, and even in plain open places it is almost impossible to discover them. In the meantime the mother feigns lameness, throws herself at your feet, kicks and gasps and flutters, to draw your attention from the chicks. The young are generally able to fly about the middle of July; but even after they can fly well they are usually advised to run and hide and lie still, no matter how closely approached, while the mother goes on with her loving, lying acting, apparently as desperately concerned for their safety as when they were featherless infants. Sometimes, however, after carefully studying the circumstances, she tells them to take wing; and up and away in a blurry birr and whir they scatter to all points of the compass, as if blown up with gunpowder, dropping cunningly out of sight three or four hundred yards off, and keeping quiet until called, after the danger is supposed to be past. If you walk on a little way without manifesting any inclination to hunt them, you may sit down at the foot of a tree near enough to see and hear the happy reunion. One touch of nature makes the whole world kin; and it is truly wonderful how love-telling the small voices of these birds are, and how far they reach through the woods into one another's hearts and into ours. The tones are so perfectly human and so full of anxious affection, few mountaineers can fail to be touched by them.

They are cared for until full grown. On the 20th of August, as I was passing along the margin of a garden spot on the head-waters of the San Joaquin, a grouse rose from the ruins of an old juniper that had been uprooted and brought down by an avalanche from a cliff overhead. She threw herself at my feet, limped and fluttered and gasped, showing, as I thought, that she had a nest and was raising a second brood. Looking for the eggs, I was surprised to see a strong-winged flock nearly as large as the mother fly up around me.

Instead of seeking a warmer climate when the winter storms set in, these hardy birds stay all the year in the High Sierra forests, and I have never known them to suffer in any sort of weather. Able to live on the buds of pine, spruce, and fir, they are forever independent in the matter of food supply, which gives so many of us trouble, dragging us here and there away from our best work. How gladly I would live on pine buds, however pitchy, for the sake of this grand independence. With all his superior resources, man makes more distracting difficulty concerning food than any other of the family.

The mountain quail or plumed partridge (*Oreortyx pictus plumiferus*) is common in all the upper portions of the park, though nowhere found in large numbers. He ranges considerably higher than the grouse in summer, but is unable to endure the heavy storms of winter. When his food is buried he descends the range to the brushy foothills, at a height of from two thousand to three thousand feet above the sea; but like every true mountaineer, he is quick to follow the spring back into the highest mountains. I think he is the very handsomest and most interesting of all the American partridges, larger and handsomer than the famous Bob White, or even the fine California valley quail or the Massena partridge of Arizona and Mexico. That he is not so regarded, is because as a lonely mountaineer he is not half known.

His plumage is delicately shaded, brown above, white and rich chestnut below and on the sides, with many dainty markings of black and white and gray here and there, while his beautiful head plume, three or four inches long, nearly straight, composed of two feathers closely folded so as to appear as one, is worn jauntily slanted backward like a single feather in a boy's cap, giving him a very marked appearance. They wander over the lonely mountains in family flocks of from six to fifteen, beneath ceanothus, manzanita, and wild cherry thickets, and over dry sandy flats, glacier meadows, rocky ridges, and beds of bryanthus around glacier lakes, especially in autumn when the berries of the upper gardens are ripe, uttering low clucking notes to enable them to keep together. When they are so suddenly disturbed that they are afraid they cannot escape the danger by running into thickets, they rise with a fine hearty whir and scatter in the brush over an area of half a square mile or so, a few of them diving into leafy trees. But as soon as the danger is past, the parents with a clear piping note call them together again. By the end of July the young are two thirds grown and fly well, though only dire necessity can compel them to try their wings. In gait, gestures, habits, and general behavior they are like domestic chickens, but infinitely finer, searching for insects and seeds, looking to this side and that, scratching among fallen leaves, jumping up to pull down grass heads, and clucking and muttering in low tones.

Once when I was seated at the foot of a tree on the head-waters of the Merced, sketching, I heard a flock up the valley behind me, and by their voices gradually sounding nearer I knew that they were feeding toward me. I kept still, hoping to see them. Soon one came within three or four feet of me, without noticing me any more than if I were a stump or a bulging part of the trunk against which I was leaning, my clothing being brown, nearly like the bark. Presently along came another and another, and it was delightful to get so near a view of these handsome chickens perfectly undisturbed, observe their manners, and hear their low peaceful notes. At last one of them caught my eye, gazed in silent wonder for a moment, then uttered a peculiar cry, which was followed by a lot of hurried muttered notes that sounded like speech. The others, of course, saw me as soon as the alarm was sounded, and joined the wonder talk, gazing and chattering, astonished but not frightened. Then all with one accord ran back with the news to the rest of the flock. "What is it? what is it? Oh, you never saw the like," they seemed to be saying. "Not a deer, or a wolf, or a bear; come see, come see." "Where? where?" "Down there by that tree." Then they approached cautiously, past the tree, stretching their necks, and looking up in turn as if knowing from the story told them just where I was. For fifteen or twenty minutes they kept coming and going, venturing within a few feet of me, and discussing the wonder in charming chatter. Their curiosity at last satisfied, they began to scatter and feed again, going back in the direction they had come from; while I, loath to part with them, followed noiselessly, crawling beneath the bushes, keeping them in sight for an hour or two, learning their habits, and finding out what seeds and berries they liked best.

The valley quail is not a mountaineer, and seldom enters the park except at a few of the lowest places on the western boundary. It belongs to the brushy foothills and plains, orchards and wheatfields, and is a hundred times more numerous than the mountain quail. It is a beautiful bird, about the size of the Bob White, and has a handsome crest of four or five feathers an inch long, recurved, standing nearly erect at times or drooping forward. The loud calls of these quails in the spring — Pe-check-ah, Pe-check-a, Hoy, Hoy — are heard far and near over all the lowlands. They have vastly increased in numbers since the settlement of the country, notwithstanding the immense numbers killed every season by boys and pot-hunters as well as the regular leggined sportsmen from the towns; for man's destructive action is more than counterbalanced by increased supply of food from cultivation, and by the destruction of their enemies — coyotes, skunks, foxes, hawks, owls, etc. — which not only kill the old birds, but plunder their nests. Where coyotes and skunks abound, scarce one pair in a hundred is successful in raising a brood. So well aware are these birds of the protection afforded by man, even now that the number of their wild enemies has been greatly diminished, that they prefer to nest near houses, notwithstanding they are so shy. Four or five pairs rear their young around our cottage every spring. One year a pair nested in a straw pile within four or five feet of the stable door, and did not leave the eggs when the men led the horses back and forth within a foot or two. For many seasons a pair nested in a tuft of pampas grass in the garden; another pair in an ivy vine on the cottage roof, and when the young were hatched, it was interesting to see the parents getting the fluffy dots down. They were greatly excited, and their anxious calls and directions to their many babes attracted our attention. They had no great dif-

ficulty in persuading the young birds to pitch themselves from the main roof to the porch roof among the ivy, but to get them safely down from the latter to the ground, a distance of ten feet, was most distressing. It seemed impossible the frail soft things could avoid being killed. The anxious parents led them to a point above a spiræa bush, that reached nearly to the eaves, which they seemed to know would break the fall. Anyhow they led their chicks to this point, and with infinite coaxing and encouragement got them to tumble themselves off. Down they rolled and sifted through the soft leaves and panicles to the pavement, and, strange to say, all got away unhurt except one that lay as if dead for a few minutes. When it revived, the joyful parents, with their brood fairly launched on the journey of life, proudly led them down the cottage hill, through the garden, and along an osage orange hedge into the cherry orchard. These charming birds even enter towns and villages, where the gardens are of good size and guns are forbidden, sometimes going several miles to feed, and returning every evening to their roosts in ivy or brushy trees and shrubs.

Geese occasionally visit the park, but never stay long. Sometimes on their way across the range, a flock wanders into Hetch-Hetchy or Yosemite to rest or get something to eat, and if shot at, are often sorely bewildered in seeking a way out. I have seen them rise from the meadow or river, wheel round in a spiral until a height of four or five hundred feet was reached, then form ranks and try to fly over the wall. But Yosemite magnitudes seem to be as deceptive to geese as to men, for they would suddenly find themselves against the cliffs not a fourth of the way to the top. Then turning in confusion, and screaming at the strange heights, they would try the opposite side, and so on, until exhausted they were compelled to rest, and only after discovering the river cañon could they make their escape. Large harrow-shaped flocks may often be seen crossing the range in the spring, at a height of at least fourteen thousand feet. Think of the strength of wing required to sustain so heavy a bird in air so thin. At this elevation it is but little over half as dense as at the sea level. Yet they hold bravely on in beautifully dressed ranks, and have breath enough to spare for loud honking. After the crest of the Sierra is passed it is only a smooth slide down the sky to the waters of Mono, where they may rest as long as they like.

Ducks of five or six species, among which are the mallard and wood duck, go far up into the heart of the mountains in the spring, and of course come down in the fall with the families they have reared. A few, as if loath to leave the mountains, pass the winter in the lower valleys of the park at a height of three thousand to four thousand feet, where the main streams are never wholly frozen over, and snow never falls to a great depth or lies long. In summer they are found up to a height of eleven thousand feet on all the lakes and branches of the rivers except the smallest, and those beside the glaciers encumbered with drifting ice and snow. I found mallards and wood ducks at Lake Tenaya, June 1, before the ice-covering was half melted, and a flock of young ones in Bloody Cañon Lake, June 20. They are usually met in pairs, never in large flocks. No place is too wild or rocky or solitary for these brave swimmers, no stream too rapid. In the roaring, resounding cañon torrents, they seem as much at home as in the tranquil reaches and lakes of the broad glacial valleys. Abandoning themselves to the wild play of the waters, they go drifting confidingly through blinding, thrashing spray, dancing on boulder-dashed waves, tossing in beautiful security on rougher water than is usually encountered by sea birds when storms are blowing.

A mother duck with her family of ten little ones, waltzing round and round in a pot-hole ornamented with foam bells, huge rocks leaning over them, cascades above and below and beside them, made one of the most interesting bird pictures I ever saw.

I have never found the great northern diver in the park lakes. Most of them are inaccessible to him. He might plump down into them, but would hardly be able to get out of them, since, with his small wings and heavy body, a wide expanse of elbow room is required in rising. Now and then one may be seen in the lower Sierra lakes to the northward about Lassens Butte and Shasta, at a height of four thousand to five thousand feet, making the loneliest places lonelier with the wildest of wild cries.

Plovers are found along the sandy shores of nearly all the mountain lakes, tripping daintily on the water's edge, picking up insects; and it is interesting to learn how few of these familiar birds are required to make a solitude cheerful.

Sandhill cranes are sometimes found in comparatively small marshes, mere dots in the mighty forest. In such spots, at an elevation of from six thousand to eight thousand feet above the sea, they are occasionally met in pairs as early as the end of May, while the snow is still deep in the surrounding fir and sugar-pine woods. And on sunny days in autumn, large flocks may be seen sailing at a great height above the forests, shaking the crisp air into rolling waves with their hearty koor-r-r, koor-r-r uck-uck, soaring in circles for hours together on their majestic wings, seeming to float without effort like clouds, eying the wrinkled landscape outspread like a map mottled with lakes and glaciers and meadows, and streaked with shadowy cañons and streams, and surveying every frog marsh and sandy flat within a hundred miles.

Eagles and hawks are oftentimes seen above the ridges and domes. The greatest height at which I have observed them was about twelve thousand feet, over the summits of Mount Hoffman, in the middle region of the park. A few pairs had their nests on the cliffs of this mountain, and could be seen every day in summer, hunting marmots, mountain beavers, pikas, etc. A pair of golden eagles have made their home in Yosemite ever since I went there thirty years ago. Their nest is on the Nevada Fall Cliff, opposite the Liberty Cap. Their screams are rather pleasant to hear in the vast gulfs between the granite cliffs, and they help the owls in keeping the echoes busy.

But of all the birds of the High Sierra, the strangest, noisiest, and most notable is the Clarke crow (*Nucifraga columbiana*). He is a foot long and nearly two feet in extent of wing, ashy gray in general color, with black wings, white tail, and a strong sharp bill, with which he digs into pine cones for the seeds on which he mainly subsists. He is quick, boisterous, jerky, and irregular in his movements and speech, and makes a tremendously loud and showy advertisement of himself, — swooping and diving in deep curves across gorges and valleys from ridge to ridge, alighting on dead spars, looking warily about him, and leaving his dry springy perches trembling from the vigor of his kick as he launches himself for a new flight, screaming from time to time loud enough to be heard more than a mile in still weather. He dwells far back on the high, storm-beaten

THE HOME OF THE EAGLE. FROM PAINTING BY THOMAS HILL.

margin of the forest, where the mountain pine, juniper, and hemlock grow wide apart on glacier pavements and domes and rough crumbling ridges, and the dwarf pine makes a low crinkled growth along the flanks of the summit peaks. In so open a region, of course, he is well seen. Everybody notices him, and nobody at first knows what to make of him. One guesses he must be a woodpecker, another a crow or some sort of jay, another a magpie. He seems to be a pretty thoroughly mixed and fermented compound of all these birds, has all their strength, cunning, shyness, thievishness, and wary, suspicious curiosity combined and condensed. He flies like a woodpecker, hammers dead limbs for insects, digs big holes in pine cones to get at the seeds, cracks nuts held between his toes, cries like a crow or Steller jay, — but in a far louder, harsher, and more forbidding tone of voice, — and besides his crow caws and screams, has a great variety of small chatter talk, mostly uttered in a fault-finding tone. Like the magpie, he steals articles that can be of no use to him. Once when I made my camp in a grove at Cathedral Lake, I chanced to leave a cake of soap on the shore where I had been washing, and a few minutes afterward I saw my soap flying past me through the grove, pushed by a Clarke crow.

In winter, when the snow is deep, the cones of the mountain pines empty, and the juniper, hemlock, and dwarf pine orchards buried, he comes down to glean seeds in the yellow pine forests, startling the grouse with his loud screams. But even in winter, in calm weather, he stays in his high mountain home, defying the bitter frost. Once I lay snowbound through a three days' storm at the timber-line on Mount Shasta ; and while the roaring snow-laden blast swept by, one of these brave birds came to my camp, and began hammering at the cones on the topmost branches of half-buried pines, without showing the slightest distress. I have seen Clarke crows feeding their young as early as June 19, at a height of more than ten thousand feet, when nearly the whole landscape was snow-covered.

They are excessively shy, and keep away from the traveler as long as they think they are observed ; but when one goes on without seeming to notice them, or sits down and keeps still, their curiosity speedily gets the better of their caution, and they come flying from tree to tree, nearer and nearer, and watch every motion. Few, I am afraid, will ever learn to like this bird, he is so suspicious and self-reliant, and his voice is so harsh that to most ears the scream of the eagle will seem melodious compared with it. Yet the mountaineer who has battled and suffered and struggled must admire his strength and endurance, — the way he faces the mountain weather, cleaves the icy blasts, cares for his young, and digs a living from the stern wilderness. Higher yet than Nucifraga dwells the little dun-headed sparrow (*Leucosticte tephrocotis*). From early spring to late autumn he is to be found only on the snowy icy peaks at the head of the glacier cirques and cañons. His feeding grounds in spring are the snow sheets between the peaks, and in midsummer and autumn the glaciers. Many bold insects go mountaineering almost as soon as they are born, ascending the highest summits on the mild breezes that blow in from the sea every day during steady weather ; but comparatively few of these adventurers find their way down or see a flower bed again. Getting tired and chilly, they alight on the snow fields and glaciers, attracted perhaps by the glare, take cold, and die. There they lie as if on a white cloth purposely outspread for them, and the dun sparrows find them a rich and varied repast requiring no pursuit, — bees and butterflies on ice, and many spicy beetles, a perpetual feast, on tables big for guests so small, and in vast banqueting halls ventilated by cool breezes that ruffle the feathers of the fairy brownies. Happy fellows, no rivals come to dispute possession with them. No other birds, not even hawks, as far as I have noticed, live so high. They see people so seldom, they flutter around the explorer with the liveliest curiosity, and come down a little way, sometimes nearly a mile, to meet him and conduct him into their icy homes.

When I was exploring the Merced group, climbing up the grand cañon between the Merced and Red mountains into the fountain amphitheatre of an ancient glacier, just as I was approaching the small active glacier that leans back in the shadow of Merced Mountain, a flock of twenty or thirty of these little birds, the first I had seen, came down the cañon to meet me, flying low, straight toward me as if they meant to fly in my face. Instead of attacking me or passing by, they circled round my head, chirping and fluttering for a minute or two, then turned and escorted me up the cañon, alighting on the nearest rocks on either hand, and flying ahead a few yards at a time to keep even with me.

I have not discovered their winter quarters. Probably they are in the desert ranges to the eastward, for I never saw any of them in Yosemite, the winter refuge of so many of the mountain birds.

Hummingbirds are among the best and most conspicuous of the mountaineers, flashing their ruby throats in countless wild gardens far up the higher slopes, where they would be least expected. All one has to do to enjoy the company of these mountain-loving midgets is to display a showy blanket or handkerchief.

The arctic bluebird is another delightful mountaineer, singing a wild, cheery song and " carrying the sky on his back " over all the gray ridges and domes of the subalpine region.

A fine, hearty, good-natured lot of woodpeckers dwell in the park, and keep it lively all the year round. Among the most notable of these are the magnificent log cock (*Ceophlœus pileatus*), the prince of Sierra woodpeckers, and only second in rank, as far as I know, of all the woodpeckers of the world ; the Lewis woodpecker, large, black, glossy, that flaps and flies like a crow, does but little hammering, and feeds in great part on wild cherries and berries ; and the carpenter, who stores up great quantities of acorns in the bark of trees for winter use. The last named species is a beautiful bird, charmingly familiar and far more common than the others. In the woods of the West he represents the eastern red-head. Bright, cheerful, industrious, not in the least shy, the carpenters give delightful animation to the open Sierra forests at a height of from three thousand to fifty-five hundred feet, especially in autumn when the acorns are ripe. Then no squirrel works harder at his pine-nut harvest than these woodpeckers at their acorn harvest, drilling holes in the thick, corky bark of the yellow pine and incense cedar, in which to store the crop for winter use ; a hole for each acorn, so nicely adjusted as to size that when the acorn, point foremost, is driven in, it fits so well that it cannot be drawn out without digging around it. Each acorn is thus carefully stored in a dry bin, perfectly protected from the weather, — a most laborious method of stowing away a crop, a granary for each kernel. Yet the birds seem never to weary at the work, but go on so diligently that they seem determined to save every acorn in the grove. They are never seen eating acorns at the time they are storing them, and it is commonly believed that they never eat them or intend to eat them, but that the wise birds store them and protect them from the depredations of squirrels and jays, solely for the sake of the worms they are supposed to contain. And because these worms are too small for use at the time the acorns drop, they are shut up like lean calves and steers, each in a separate stall with abundance of food, to grow big and fat by the time they will be most wanted, that is, in winter, when insects are scarce and stall-fed worms most valuable. So these woodpeckers are supposed to be a sort of cattle-raisers, each with a drove of thousands, rivaling the ants that raise grain and keep herds of plant lice for milk cows. Needless to say the story is not true, though some naturalists even believe it. When Emerson was in the park, having heard the worm story and seen the great pines plugged full of acorns. he asked (just to pump me,

I suppose), "Why do the woodpeckers take the trouble to put acorns into the bark of the trees?" "For the same reason," I replied, "that bees store honey and squirrels nuts." "But they tell me, Mr. Muir, that woodpeckers don't eat acorns." "Yes, they do," I said, "I have seen them eating them. During snowstorms they seem to eat little besides acorns. I have repeatedly interrupted them at their meals, and seen the perfectly sound, half-eaten acorns. They eat them in the shell as some people eat eggs." "But what about the worms?" "I suppose," I said, "that when they come to a wormy one they eat both worm and acorn. Anyhow, they eat the sound ones when they can't find anything they like better, and from the time they store them until they are used they guard them, and woe to the squirrel or jay caught stealing." Indians, in times of scarcity, frequently resort to these stores and chop them out with hatchets; a bushel or more may be gathered from a single cedar or pine.

The common robin, with all his familiar notes and gestures, is found nearly everywhere throughout the park, — in shady dells beneath dogwoods and maples, along the flowery banks of the streams, tripping daintily about the margins of meadows in the fir and pine woods, and far beyond on the shores of glacier lakes and the slopes of the peaks. How admirable the constitution and temper of this cheery, graceful bird, keeping glad health over so vast and varied a range. In all America he is at home, flying from plains to mountains up and down, north and south, away and back, with the seasons and supply of food. Oftentimes, in the High Sierra, as you wander through the solemn woods, awe-stricken and silent, you will hear the reassuring voice of this fellow wanderer ringing out sweet and clear as if saying, "Fear not, fear not. Only love is here." In the severest solitudes he seems as happy as in gardens and apple orchards.

The robins enter the park as soon as the snow melts, and go on up the mountains, gradually higher, with the opening flowers, until the topmost glacier meadows are reached in June and July. After the short summer is done, they descend like most other summer visitors in concord with the weather, keeping out of the first heavy snows as much as possible, while lingering among the frost-nipped wild cherries on the slopes just below the glacier meadows. Thence they go to the lower slopes of the forest region, compelled to make haste at times by heavy all-day storms, picking up seeds or benumbed insects by the way, and at last all, save a few that winter in Yosemite valleys, arrive in the vineyards and orchards and stubble-fields of the lowlands in November, picking up fallen fruit and grain, and awakening old-time memories among the white-headed pioneers, who cannot fail to recognize the influence of so homelike a bird. They are then in flocks of hundreds, and make their way into the gardens of towns as well as into the parks and fields and orchards about the bay of San Francisco, where many of the wanderers are shot for sport and the morsel of meat on their breasts. Man then seems a beast of prey. Not even genuine piety can make the robin-killer quite respectable. Saturday is the great slaughter day in the bay region. Then the city pot-hunters, with a ragtag of boys, go forth to kill, kept in countenance by a sprinkling of regular sportsmen arrayed in self-conscious majesty and leggins, leading dogs and carrying hammerless, breech-loading guns of famous makers. Over the fine landscapes the killing goes forward with shameful enthusiasm. After escaping countless dangers, thousands fall, big bagfuls are gathered, many are left wounded to die slowly, no Red Cross Society to help them. Next day, Sunday, the blood and leggins vanish from the most devout of the bird butchers, who go to church, carrying gold-headed canes instead of guns. After hymns, prayers, and sermon they go home to feast, to put God's songbirds to use, put them in their dinners instead of in their hearts, eat them, and suck the pitiful little drumsticks. It is only race living on race, to be sure, but Christians singing Divine Love need not be driven to such straits while wheat and apples grow and the shops are full of dead cattle. Songbirds for food! Compared with this, making kindlings of pianos and violins would be pious economy.

The larks come in large flocks from the hills and mountains in the fall, and are slaughtered as ruthlessly as the robins. Fortunately, most of our songbirds keep back in leafy hidings, and are comparatively inaccessible.

The water ouzel, in his rocky home amid foaming waters, seldom sees a gun, and of all the singers I like him the best. He is a plainly dressed little bird, about the size of a robin, with short, crisp, but rather broad wings, and a tail of moderate length, slanted up, giving him with his nodding, bobbing manners a wrennish look. He is usually seen fluttering about in the spray of falls and the rapid cascading portions of the main branches of the rivers. These are his favorite haunts; but he is often seen also on comparatively level reaches and occasionally on the shores of mountain lakes, especially at the beginning of winter, when heavy snowfalls have blurred the streams with sludge. Though not a water bird in structure, he gets his living in the water, and is never seen away from the immediate margin of streams. He dives fearlessly into rough, boiling eddies and rapids to feed at the bottom, flying under water seemingly as easily as in the air. Sometimes he wades in shallow places, thrusting his head under from time to time in a nodding, frisky way that is sure to attract attention. His flight is a solid whir of wing-beats like that of a partridge, and in going from place to place along his favorite string of rapids he follows the windings of the stream, and usually alights on some rock or snag on the bank or out in the current, or rarely on the dry limb of an overhanging tree, perching like a tree bird when it suits his convenience. He has the oddest, neatest manners imaginable, and all his gestures as he flits about in the wild, dashing waters bespeak the utmost cheerfulness and confidence. He sings both winter and summer, in all sorts of weather, — a sweet, fluty melody, rather low, and much less keen and accentuated than from the brisk vigor of his movements one would be led to expect.

How romantic and beautiful is the life of this brave little singer on the wild mountain streams, building his round bossy nest of moss by the side of a rapid or fall, where it is sprinkled and kept fresh and green by the spray! No wonder he sings well, since all the air about him is music; every breath he draws is part of a song, and he gets his first music lessons before he is born; for the eggs vibrate in time with the tones of the waterfalls. Bird and stream are inseparable, songful and wild, gentle and strong, — the bird ever in danger in the midst of the stream's mad whirlpools, yet seeming immortal. And so I might go on, writing words, words, words; but to what purpose? Go see him and love him, and through him as through a window look into Nature's warm heart.

WATER-OUSEL.

Gorge of the Merced, from Glacier Point Trail.

THE FOUNTAINS AND STREAMS OF THE YOSEMITE NATIONAL PARK.

THE joyful, songful streams of the Sierra are among the most famous and interesting in the world, and draw the admiring traveler on and on through their wonderful cañons, year after year, unwearied. After long wanderings with them, tracing them to their fountains, learning their history and the forms they take in their wild works and ways throughout the different seasons of the year, we may then view them together in one magnificent show, outspread over all the range like embroidery, their silvery branches interlacing on a thousand mountains, singing their way home to the sea: the small rills, with hard roads to travel, dropping from ledge to ledge, pool to pool, like chains of sweet-toned bells, slipping gently over beds of pebbles and sand, resting in lakes, shining, spangling, shimmering, lapping the shores with whispering ripples, and shaking overleaning bushes and grass; the larger streams and rivers in the cañons displaying noble purity and beauty with ungovernable energy, rushing down smooth inclines in wide foamy sheets, fold over fold, springing up here and there in magnificent whirls scattering crisp clashing spray for the sunbeams to iris, bursting with hoarse reverberating roar through rugged gorges and boulder dams, booming in falls, gliding, glancing, with cool soothing murmuring, through long forested reaches richly embowered, — filling the grand cañons with glorious song, and giving life to all the landscape.

The present rivers of the Sierra are still young, and have made but little mark as yet on the grand cañons prepared for them by the ancient glaciers. Only a very short geological time ago they all lay buried beneath the glaciers they drained, singing in low smothered or silvery ringing tones in crystal channels, while the summer weather melted the ice and snow of the surface or gave showers. At first only in warm weather was any part of these buried rivers displayed in the light of day; for as soon as frost prevailed the surface rills vanished, though the streams beneath the ice and in the body of it flowed on all the year.

When, toward the close of the glacial period, the ice mantle began to shrink and recede from the lowlands, the lower portions of the rivers were developed, issuing from cavelike openings on the melting margin, and growing longer as the ice withdrew; while for many a century the tributaries and upper portions of the trunks remained covered. In the fullness of time these also were set free in the sunshine, to take their places in the newborn landscapes; each tributary with its smaller branches being gradually developed like the main trunks, as the climatic changes went on. At first all of them were muddy with glacial detritus, and they became clear only after the glaciers they drained had receded beyond lake basins in which the sediments were dropped.

This early history is clearly explained by the present rivers of southeastern Alaska. Of those draining glaciers that discharge into arms of the sea, only the rills on the surface of the ice, and upboiling, eddying, turbid currents in the tide water in front of the terminal ice wall, are visible. Where glaciers, in the first stage of decadence, have receded from the shore, short sections of the trunks of the rivers that are to take their places may be seen rushing out from caverns and tunnels in the melting front, — rough, roaring, detritus-laden torrents, foaming and tumbling over outspread terminal moraines to the sea, perhaps without a single bush or flower to brighten their raw, shifting banks.

Again, in some of the warmer cañons and valleys from which the trunk glaciers have been melted, the main trunks of the rivers are well developed, and their banks planted with fine forests, while their upper branches, lying high on the snowy mountains, are still buried beneath shrinking residual glaciers; illustrating every stage of development, from icy darkness to light, and from muddiness to crystal clearness.

Now that the hard grinding sculpture work of the glacial period is done, the whole bright band of Sierra rivers run clear all the year, except when the snow is melting fast in the warm spring weather, and during extraordinary winter floods and the heavy thunderstorms of summer called cloud-bursts. Even then they are not muddy above the foothill mining region, unless the moraines have been loosened and the vegetation destroyed by sheep; for the rocks of the upper basins are clean, and the most able streams find but little to carry save the spoils of the forests, — trees, branches, flakes of bark, cones, leaves, pollen dust, etc., — with scales of mica, sand grains, and boulders, which are rolled along the bottom of the steep parts of the main channels. Short sections of a few of the highest tributaries heading in glaciers are of course turbid with finely ground rock mud, but this is dropped in the first lakes they enter.

On the northern part of the range, mantled with porous fissured volcanic rocks, the fountain waters sink and flow below the surface for considerable distances, groping their way in the dark like the draining streams of glaciers, and at last bursting forth in big generous springs, filtered and cool and exquisitely clear. Some of the largest look like lakes, their waters welling straight up from the bottom of deep rock basins in quiet massive volume giving rise to young rivers. Others issue from horizontal clefts in sheer bluffs, with loud tumultuous roaring that may be heard half a mile or more. Magnificent examples of these great northern spring fountains, twenty or thirty feet deep and ten to nearly a hundred yards wide, abound on the main branches of the Feather, Pitt, McCloud, and Fall rivers.

The springs of the Yosemite Park, and the high Sierra in general, though many times more numerous, are comparatively small, oozing from moraines and snowbanks in thin, flat, irregular currents which remain on the surface or near it, the rocks of the south half of the range being mostly flawless impervious granite; and since granite is but slightly soluble, the streams are particularly pure. Nevertheless, though they are all clear, and in the upper and main central forest regions delightfully lively and cool, they vary somewhat in color and taste as well as temperature, on account of differences, however slight, in exposure, and in the rocks and vegetation with which they come in contact. Some are more exposed than others to winds and sunshine in their falls and thin plumelike cascades; the amount of dashing, mixing, and airing the waters of each receive varies considerably; and there is always more or less variety in the kind and quantity of the vegetation they flow through, and in the time they lie in shady or sunny lakes and bogs.

The water of one of the branches of the north fork of Owens River, near the southeastern boundary of the park, at an elevation of ninety-five hundred feet above the sea, is the best I ever found. It is not only delightfully cool and bright, but brisk, sparkling, exhilarating, and so positively delicious to the taste that a party of friends I led to it twenty-five years ago still praise it, and refer to it as "that wonderful champagne water;" though, comparatively, the finest wine is a coarse and vulgar drink. The party camped about a week in a pine grove on the edge of a little round sedgy meadow through which the stream ran bank full, and drank its icy water on frosty morn-

Bridal-Veil Fall.

ings, before breakfast, and at night about as eagerly as in the heat of the day; lying down and taking massy draughts direct from the brimming flood, lest the touch of a cup might disturb its celestial flavor. On one of my excursions I took pains to trace this stream to its head springs. It is mostly derived from snow that lies in heavy drifts and avalanche heaps on or near the axis of the range. It flows first in flat sheets over coarse sand or shingle derived from a granite ridge and the metamorphic slates of Red Mountain. Then, gathering its many small branches, it runs through beds of moraine material, and a series of lakelets and meadows and frosty juicy bogs bordered with heathworts and linked together by short bouldery reaches. Below these, growing strong with tribute drawn from many a snowy fountain on either side, the glad stream goes dashing and swirling through clumps of the white-barked pine, and tangled willow and alder thickets enriched by the fragrant herbaceous vegetation usually found about them. And just above the level camp meadow it is chafed and churned and beaten white over and over again in crossing a talus of big earthquake boulders, giving it a very thorough airing. But to what the peculiar indefinable excellence of this water is due I don't know; for other streams in adjacent cañons are aired in about the same way, and draw traces of minerals and plant essences from similar sources. The best mineral water yet discovered in the park flows from the Tuolumne soda springs, on the north side of the Big Meadow. Mountaineers like it and ascribe every healing virtue to it, but in no way can any of these waters be compared with the Owens River champagne.

It is a curious fact that the waters of some of the Sierra lakes and streams are invisible, or nearly so, under certain weather conditions. This is noticed by mountaineers, hunters, and prospectors, wide-awake, sharp-eyed observers, little likely to be fooled by fine whims. One of these mountain men, whom I had nursed while a broken leg was mending, always gratefully reported the wonders he found. Once, returning from a trip on the head waters of the Tuolumne, he came running eagerly, crying: "Muir, I 've found the queerest lake in the mountains! It 's high up where nothing grows; and when it is n't shiny you can't see it, and you walk right into it as if there was nothing there. The first you know of that lake you are in it, and get tripped up by the water, and hear the splash." The waters of Illilouette Creek are nearly invisible in the autumn; so that, in following the channel, jumping from boulder to boulder after a shower, you will frequently drag your feet in the apparently surfaceless pools.

Excepting a few low warm slopes, fountain snow usually covers all the Yosemite Park from November or December to May, most of it until June or July, while on the coolest parts of the north slopes of the mountains, at a height of eleven to thirteen thousand feet, it is perpetual. It seldom lies at a greater depth than two or three feet on the lower margin, ten feet over the middle forested region, or fifteen to twenty feet in the shadowy cañons and cirques among the peaks of the summit, except where it is drifted, or piled in avalanche heaps at the foot of long converging slopes to form perennial fountains.

The first crop of snow crystals that whitens the mountains and refreshes the streams usually falls in September or October, in the midst of charming Indian-summer weather, often while the goldenrods and gentians are in their prime; but these Indian-summer snows, like some of the late ones that bury the June gardens, vanish in a day or two, and garden work goes on with accelerated speed. The grand winter storms that load the mountains with enduring fountain snow seldom set in before the end of November. The fertile clouds, descending, glide about and hover in brooding silence, as if thoughtfully examining the forests and streams with reference to the work before them; then small flakes or single crystals appear, glinting and swirling in zigzags and spirals; and soon the thronging feathery masses fill the sky and make darkness like night, hurrying wandering mountaineers to their winter quarters. The first fall is usually about two to four feet deep. Then, with intervals of bright weather, not very cold, storm succeeds storm, heaping snow on snow, until from thirty to fifty or sixty feet has fallen; but on account of heavy settling and compacting, and the waste from evaporation and melting, the depth in the middle region, as stated above, rarely exceeds ten feet. Evaporation never wholly ceases, even in the coldest weather, and the sunshine between storms melts the surface more or less. Waste from melting also goes on at the bottom from summer heat stored in the rocks, as is shown by the rise of the streams after the first general storm, and their steady sustained flow all winter.

In the deep sugar-pine and silver-fir woods, up to a height of eight thousand feet, most of the snow lies where it falls, in one smooth universal fountain, until set free in the streams. But in the lighter forests of the two-leaved pine, and on the bleak slopes above the timber line, there is much wild drifting during storms accompanied by high winds, and for a day or two after they have fallen, when the temperature is low, and the snow dry and dusty. Then the trees, bending in the darkening blast, roar like feeding lions; the frozen lakes are buried; so also are the streams, which now flow in dark tunnels, as if another glacial period had come. On high ridges, where the winds have a free sweep, magnificent overcurling cornices are formed, which, with the avalanche piles, last as fountains almost all summer; and when an exceptionally high wind is blowing from the north, the snow, rolled, drifted, and ground to dust, is driven up the converging northern slopes of the peaks, and sent flying for miles in the form of bright wavering banners, displayed in wonderful clearness and beauty against the sky.

The greatest storms, however, are usually followed by a deep peculiar silence, especially profound and solemn in the forests, and the noble trees stand hushed and motionless, as if under a spell, until the morning sunbeams begin to sift through their laden spires. Then the snow, shifting and falling from the top branches, strikes the lower ones in succession, and dislodges bossy masses all the way down. Thus each tree is enveloped in a hollow conical avalanche of fairy fineness, silvery white, irised on the outside; while the relieved branches spring up and wave with startling effect in the general stillness, as if moving of their own volition. These beautiful tree avalanches, hundreds of which may be seen falling at once on fine mornings after storms, pile their snow in raised rings around corresponding hollows beneath the trees, making the forest mantle somewhat irregular, but without greatly influencing its duration and the flow of the streams.

The large storm avalanches are most abundant on the summit peaks of the range. They descend the broad steep slopes, as well as narrow gorges and

THE YOSEMITE FALL.

couloirs, with grand roaring and booming, and glide in graceful curves out on the glaciers they so bountifully feed.

Down in the main cañons of the middle region broad masses are launched over the brows of cliffs three or four thousand feet high, which, worn to dust by friction in falling so far through the air, oftentimes hang for a minute or two in front of the tremendous precipices like gauzy half-transparent veils, gloriously beautiful when the sun is shining through them. Most of the cañon avalanches, however, flow in regular channels, like the cascades of tributary streams. When the snow first gives way on the upper slopes of their basins a dull muffled rush and rumble is heard, which, increasing with heavy deliberation, seems to draw rapidly nearer with appalling intensity of tone. Presently the wild flood comes in sight, bounding out over bosses and sheer places, leaping from bench to bench, spreading and narrowing and throwing off clouds of whirling diamond dust like a majestic foamy cataract. Compared with cascades and falls, avalanches are short-lived, and the sharp clashing sounds so common in dashing water are usually wanting; but in their deep thunder tones and pearly purple-tinged whiteness, and in dress, gait, gestures, and general behavior, they are much alike.

Besides these common storm avalanches there are two other kinds, the annual and the century, which still further enrich the scenery, though their influence on fountains is comparatively small. Annual avalanches are composed of heavy compacted snow which has been subjected to frequent alternations of frost and thaw. They are developed on cañon and mountain sides, the greater number of them, at elevations of from nine to ten thousand feet, where the slopes are so inclined that the dry snows of winter accumulate and hold fast until the spring thaws sap their foundations and make them slippery. Then away in grand style go the ponderous icy masses adorned with crystalline spray, without any cloudy snow dust; some of the largest descending more than a mile with even sustained energy and directness like thunderbolts. The grand century avalanches, that mow wide swaths through the upper forests, occur on shady mountain sides about ten to twelve thousand feet high, where, under ordinary conditions, the snow accumulated from winter to winter lies at rest

GOD'S TENTS—AFTER A SNOW STORM.

for many years, allowing trees fifty to a hundred feet high to grow undisturbed on the slopes below them. On their way through the forests they usually make a clean sweep, stripping off the soil as well as the trees, clearing paths two or three hundred yards wide from the timber line to the glacier meadows, and piling the uprooted trees, head downward, in windrows along the sides like lateral moraines. Scars and broken branches on the standing trees bordering the gaps record the side depth of the overwhelming flood; and when we come to count the annual wood rings of the uprooted trees, we learn that some of these colossal avalanches occur only once in about a century, or even at still wider intervals.

Few mountaineers go far enough, during the snowy months, to see many avalanches, and fewer still know the thrilling exhilaration of riding on them. In all my wild mountaineering I have enjoyed only one avalanche ride; and the start was so sudden, and the end came so soon, I thought but little of the danger that goes with this sort of travel, though one thinks fast at such times. One calm, bright morning in Yosemite, after a hearty storm had given three or four feet of fresh snow to the mountains, being eager to see as many avalanches as possible, and gain wide views of the peaks and forests, arrayed in their new robes, before the sunshine had time to change or rearrange them, I set out early to climb by a side cañon to the top of a commanding ridge a little over three thousand feet above the valley. On account of the looseness of the snow that blocked the cañon I knew the climb would be trying, and estimated it might require three or four hours. But it proved far more difficult than I had foreseen. Most of the way I sank waist-deep, in some places almost out of sight; and after spending the day to within half an hour of sundown in this loose, baffling snow work, I was still several hundred feet below the summit. Then my hopes were reduced to getting up in time for the sunset, and a quick, sparkling home-going beneath the stars. But I was not to get top views of any sort that day; for deep trampling near the cañon head, where the snow was strained, started an avalanche, and I was swished back down to the foot of the cañon as if by enchantment. The plodding, wallowing ascent of about a mile had taken all day, the undoing descent perhaps a minute. When the snow suddenly gave way, I instinctively threw myself on my back and spread my arms, to try to keep from sinking. Fortunately, though the grade of the cañon was steep, it was not interrupted by step levels or precipices big enough to cause outbounding or free plunging. On no part of the rush was I buried. I was only moderately imbedded on the surface or a little below it, and covered with a hissing back-streaming veil of dusty snow particles; and as the whole mass beneath or about me joined in the flight I felt no friction, though tossed here and there, and lurched from side to side. And when the torrent swedged and came to rest I found myself on the top of the crumpled pile, without a single bruise or scar. Hawthorne says that steam has spiritualized travel, notwithstanding the smoke, friction smells, and clatter of boat and rail riding. This flight in a milky way of snow flowers was the most spiritual of all my travels; and, after many years, the mere thought of it is still an exhilaration.

In the spring, after all the avalanches are down and the snow is melting fast, it is glorious to hear the streams sing out on the mountains. Every fountain swelling, countless rills hurry together to the rivers at the call of the sun; beginning to run and sing soon after sunrise, increasing until toward sundown, then gradually failing through the cold frosty hours of the night. Thus the volume of the upper rivers, even in flood time, is nearly doubled during the day, rising and falling as regularly as the tides of the sea. At the height of flood, in the warmest June weather, they seem fairly to shout for joy, and clash their upleaping waters together like clapping of hands; racing down the cañons with white manes flying in glorious exuberance of strength, compelling huge sleeping boulders to wake up and join in the dance and song to swell their chorus.

Then the plants also are in flood; the hidden sap singing into leaf and flower, responding as faithfully to the call of the sun as the streams from the snow, gathering along the outspread roots like rills in their channels on the mountains, rushing up the stems of herb and tree, swirling in their myriad cells like streams in potholes, spreading along the branches and breaking into foamy bloom, while fragrance, like a finer music, rises and flows with the winds.

About the same may be said of the spring gladness of blood when the red streams surge and sing in accord with

Foot of Sentinel Fall

the swelling plants and rivers, inclining animals and everybody to travel in hurrahing crowds like floods, while exhilarating melody in color and fragrance, form and motion, flows to the heart through all the quickening senses.

In early summer the streams are in bright prime, running crystal clear, deep and full, but not overflowing their banks, — about as deep through the night as the day, the variation so marked in spring being now too slight to be noticed. Nearly all the weather is cloudless sunshine, and everything is at its brightest, — lake, river, garden, and forest, with all their warm throbbing life. Most of the plants are in full leaf and flower; the blessed ousels have built their mossy huts, and are now singing their sweetest songs on spray-sprinkled ledges beside the waterfalls.

In tranquil, mellow autumn, when the year's work is about done, when the fruits are ripe, birds and seeds out of their nests, and all the landscape is glowing like a benevolent countenance at rest, then the streams are at their lowest ebb, — their wild rejoicing soothed to thoughtful calm. All the smaller tributaries, whose branches do not reach back to the perennial fountains of the summit peaks, shrink to whispering, tinkling currents. The snow of their basins gone, they are now fed only by small moraine springs, whose waters are mostly evaporated in passing over warm pavements, and in feeling their way from pool to pool through the midst of boulders and sand. Even the main streams are so low they may be easily forded, and their grand falls and cascades, now gentle and approachable, have waned to sheets and webs of embroidery, falling fold over fold in new and ever changing beauty.

Two of the most songful of the rivers, the Tuolumne and Merced, water nearly all the park, spreading their branches far and wide, like broad-headed oaks; and the highest branches of each draw their sources from one and the same fountain on Mount Lyell, at an elevation of about thirteen thousand feet above the sea. The crest of the mountain, against which the head of the glacier rests, is worn to a thin blade full of joints, through which a part of the glacial water flows southward, giving rise to the highest trickling affluents of the Merced; while the main drainage, flowing northward, gives rise to those of the Tuolumne. After diverging for a distance of ten or twelve miles these twin rivers flow in a general westerly direction, descending rapidly for the first thirty miles, and rushing in glorious apron cascades and falls from one Yosemite valley to another. Below the Yosemites they descend in gray rapids and swirling, swaying reaches, through the chaparral-clad cañons of the foothills and across the golden California plain, to their confluence with the San Joaquin, where, after all their long wanderings, they are only about ten miles apart.

Merced Gorge.

The main cañons are from fifty to seventy miles long, and from two to four thousand feet deep, carved in the solid flank of the range. Though rough in some places and hard to travel, they are the most delightful of roads, leading through the grandest scenery, full of life and motion, and offering most telling lessons in earth sculpture. The walls, far from being unbroken, featureless cliffs, seem like ranges of separate mountains, so deep and varied is their sculpture; rising in lordly domes, towers, round-browed outstanding headlands, and clustering spires, with dark shadowy side cañons between. But, however wonderful in height and mass and fineness of finish, no anomalous curiosities are presented, no "freaks of nature." All stand related in delicate rhythm, a grand glacial rock song. Among the most interesting and influential of the secondary features of cañon scenery are the great avalanche taluses, that lean against the walls at intervals of a mile or two. In the middle Yosemite region they are usually from three to five hundred feet high, and are made up of huge angular well-preserved unshifting boulders, overgrown with gray lichens, trees, shrubs, and delicate flowering plants. Some of the largest of the boulders are forty or fifty feet cube, weighing from five to ten thousand tons; and where the cleavage joints of the granite are exceptionally wide apart a few blocks may be found nearly a hundred feet in diameter. These wonderful boulder piles are distributed throughout all the cañons of the range, completely choking them in some of the narrower portions, and no mountaineer will be likely to forget the savage roughness of the roads they make. Even the swift overbearing rivers, accustomed to sweep everything out of their way, are in some places bridled and held in check by them. Foaming, roaring, in glorious majesty of flood, rushing off long rumbling trains of ponderous blocks without apparent effort, they are not able to move the largest, which, withstanding all assaults for centuries, are left at rest in the channels, like islands, with gardens on their tops, fringed with foam below, with flowers above.

On some points concerning the origin of these taluses I was long in doubt. Plainly enough they were derived from the cliffs above them, the size of each talus being approximately measured by a scar on the wall, the rough angular surface of which contrasts with the rounded, glaciated, unfractured parts. I saw also that, instead of being slowly accumulated material, weathered off boulder by boulder in the ordinary way, almost every talus had been formed suddenly, in a single avalanche, and had not been increased in size during the last three or four centuries; for trees three or four hundred years old were growing on them, some standing at the top close to the wall, without a bruise or broken branch, showing that scarcely a single boulder had fallen among them since they were planted. Furthermore, all the taluses throughout the range seemed, by the trees and lichens growing on them, to be of the same age. All the phenomena pointed straight to a grand ancient earthquake. But I left the question open for years, and went on from cañon to cañon, observing again and again; measuring the heights of taluses throughout the range on both flanks, and the variations in the angles of their surface slopes; studying the way their boulders were assorted and related and brought to rest, and the cleavage joints of the cliffs from whence they were derived, cautious about making up my mind. Only after I had seen one made did all doubt as to their formation vanish.

In Yosemite Valley, one morning about two o'clock, I was aroused by an earthquake; and though I had never before enjoyed a storm of this sort, the strange wild thrilling motion and rumbling could not be mistaken, and I ran out of my cabin, near the Sentinel Rock, both glad and frightened, shouting, "A noble earthquake!" feeling sure I was going to learn something. The shocks were so violent and varied, and succeeded one another so closely, one had to balance in walking as if on the deck of a ship among waves, and it seemed impossible the high cliffs should escape being shattered. In particular, I feared that the sheer-fronted Sentinel Rock, which rises to a height of three thousand feet, would be shaken down, and I took shelter back of a big pine, hoping I might be protected from outbounding boulders, should any come so far. I was now convinced that an earthquake had been the maker of the taluses, and positive proof soon came. It was a calm moonlight night, and no sound was heard for the first minute or two save a low muffled underground rumbling and a slight rustling of the agitated trees, as if, in wrestling with the mountains, Nature were holding her breath. Then, suddenly, out of the strange silence and strange motion there came a tremendous roar. The Eagle Rock, a short distance up the valley, had given way, and I saw it falling in thousands of the great boulders I had been studying so long, pouring to the valley floor in a free curve luminous from friction, making a terribly sublime and beautiful spectacle, — an arc of fire fifteen hundred feet span, as true in form and as steady as a rainbow, in the midst of the stupendous roaring rockstorm. The sound was inconceivably deep and broad and earnest, as if the whole earth, like a living creature, had at last found a voice, and were calling to her sister planets. It seemed to me that if all the thunder I ever heard were condensed into one roar it would not equal this rock

Sentinel Rock and Fall.

roar at the birth of a mountain talus. Think, then, of the roar that arose to heaven when all the thousands of ancient cañon taluses throughout the length and breadth of the range were simultaneously given birth!

The main storm was soon over, and, eager to see the newborn talus, I ran up the valley in the moonlight and climbed it before the huge blocks, after their wild fiery flight, had come to complete rest. They were slowly settling into their places, chafing, grating against one another, groaning and whispering; but no motion was visible except in a stream of small fragments pattering down the face of the cliff at the head of the talus. A cloud of dust particles, the smallest of the boulders, floated out across the whole breadth of the valley and formed a ceiling that lasted until after sunrise; and the air was loaded with the odor of crushed Douglas spruces, from a grove that had been mowed down and mashed like weeds.

Sauntering about to see what other changes had been made, I found the Indians in the middle of the valley, terribly frightened, of course, fearing the angry spirits of the rocks were trying to kill them. The few whites wintering in the valley were assembled in front of the old Hutchings Hotel, comparing notes and meditating flight to steadier ground, seemingly as sorely frightened as the Indians. It is always interesting to see people in dead earnest, from whatever cause, and earthquakes make everybody earnest. Shortly after sunrise, a low blunt muffled rumbling, like distant thunder, was followed by another series of shocks, which, though not nearly so severe as the first, made the cliffs and domes tremble like jelly, and the big pines and oaks thrill and swish and wave their branches with startling effect. Then the groups of talkers were suddenly hushed, and the solemnity on their faces was sublime. One in particular of these winter neighbors, a rather thoughtful, speculative man, with whom I had often conversed, was a firm believer in the cataclysmic origin of the valley, and I now jokingly remarked that his wild tumble-down-and-engulfment hypothesis might soon be proved, since these underground rumblings and shakings might be the forerunners of another Yosemite-making cataclysm, which would perhaps double the depth of the valley by swallowing the floor, leaving the ends of the wagon roads and trails three or four thousand feet in the air. Just then came the second series of shocks, and it was fine to see how awfully silent and solemn he became. His belief in the existence of a mysterious abyss, into which the suspended floor of the valley and all the domes and battlements of the walls might at any moment go roaring down, mightily troubled him. To cheer and tease him into another view of the case, I said: "Come, cheer up; smile a little and clap your hands, now that kind Mother Earth is trotting us on her knee to amuse us and make us good." But the well-meant joke seemed irreverent and utterly failed, as if only prayerful terror could rightly belong to the wild beauty-making business. Even after all the heavier shocks were over, I could do nothing to reassure him. On the contrary, he handed me the keys of his little store, and, with a companion of like mind, fled to the lowlands. In about a month he returned; but a sharp shock occurred that very day, which sent him flying again.

The rocks trembled more or less every day for over two months, and I kept a bucket of water on my table, to learn what I could of the movements. The blunt thunder tones in the depths of the mountains were usually followed by sudden jarring horizontal thrusts from the northward, often succeeded by twisting, upjolting movements. Judging by its effects, this Yosemite, or Inyo earthquake, as it is sometimes called, was gentle as compared with the one that gave

TENAYA CANON, FROM GLACIER POINT.

rise to the grand talus system of the range and did so much for the cañon scenery. Nature, usually so deliberate in her operations, then created, as we have seen, a new set of features, simply by giving the mountains a shake, — changing not only the high peaks and cliffs, but the streams. As soon as these rock avalanches fell every stream began to sing new songs; for in many places thousands of boulders were hurled into their channels, roughening and half damming them, compelling the waters to surge and roar in rapids where before they were gliding smoothly. Some of the streams were completely dammed, driftwood, leaves, etc., filling the interstices between the boulders, thus giving rise to lakes and level reaches; and these, again, after being gradually filled in, to smooth meadows, through which the streams now silently meander; while at the same time some of the taluses took the places of old meadows and groves. Thus rough places were made smooth, and smooth places rough. But on the whole, by what at first sight seemed pure confusion and ruin, the landscapes were enriched; for gradually every talus, however big the boulders composing it, was covered with groves and gardens, and made a finely proportioned and ornamental base for the sheer cliffs. In this beauty work, every boulder is prepared and measured and put in its place more thoughtfully than are the stones of temples. If for a moment you are inclined to regard these taluses as mere draggled, chaotic dumps, climb to the top of one of them, tie your mountain shoes firmly over the instep, and with braced nerves run down without any haggling, puttering hesitation, boldly jumping from boulder to boulder with even speed. You will then find your feet playing a tune, and quickly discover the music and poetry of rock piles, — a fine lesson; and all nature's wildness tells the same story. Storms of every sort, torrents, earthquakes, cataclysms, "convulsions of nature," etc., however mysterious and lawless at first sight they may seem, are only harmonious notes in the song of creation, varied expressions of God's love.

CATHEDRAL ROCK.